When Daddy Comes Home

Toni Maguire

When Daddy Comes Home

HARPER
element

HarperElement
An Imprint of HarperCollins*Publishers*
77–85 Fulham Palace Road,
Hammersmith, London W6 8JB

The website address is: www.thorsonselement.com

and *HarperElement* are trademarks
of HarperCollins*Publishers* Ltd

First published by HarperElement 2007

1 3 5 7 9 10 8 6 4 2

© Toni Maguire 2007

Toni Maguire asserts the moral right to be
identified as the author of this work

A catalogue record of this book is
available from the British Library

HB ISBN-13 978-0-00-724398-3
HB ISBN-10 0-00-724398-7
PB ISBN-13 978-0-00-724399-0
PB ISBN-10 0-00-724399-5

Printed and bound in Great Britain by
Clays Ltd, St Ives plc

This book is a work of non-fiction based on the recollections
of Toni Maguire. The names of people, places, dates and the detail of events
have been changed to protect the privacy of others. The author has warranted to the
publishers that, except in such minor respects not affecting the substantial accuracy
of the work, the contents of this book are true.

This book is proudly printed on paper which contains wood
from well-managed forests, certified in accordance with
the rules of the Forest Stewardship Council.
For more information about FSC.
please visit www.fsc-uk.org

Mixed Sources
Product group from well-managed
forests and other controlled sources
www.fsc.org Cert no. SW-COC-1806
© 1996 Forest Stewardship Council
FSC

To Alison Pierce.
For thirty years of love and friendship.
Through the worst of times and the best of times.

Acknowledgements

Special thanks to my agent Barbara Levy and to Marian Sweet for her understanding and humour.

A big thank you to Carole Tonkinson and Kirsty Crawford plus all the HarperCollins team for their efforts on both my books.

The soul of a childhood departs quietly without fuss or trouble.
The little girl it had belonged to did not understand where it had
*   gone or why it had left her.*
But she missed it, for with its absence she was lonely.

Chapter One

'I'm an adult now, the past is dealt with.'

That was what I told myself as I stood at the desk where my mother had done her household accounts.

The voice of my subconscious mocked me then.

'The past is never dealt with, Toni. It's our past that creates us.'

No sooner did those unwanted words flit into my head than my treacherous memories began to slide back to when I was the teenage Antoinette.

Antoinette. Just the name filled me with sadness.

I pushed those thoughts to the back of my mind and opened the desk, the only piece of furniture that remained from the joint home my parents had shared. I found the deeds of the house and put them to one side ready to give to the solicitor. Next came an old leather wallet which, on opening it, I saw contained two hundred pounds in notes of various denominations.

Underneath them, I found letters yellowed by age and three photographs that must have lain there from before my mother's death. One was of my mother and me when I was just under a year old, one was of my mother's parents and there was a head-and-shoulder photograph of my grandmother when she was around thirty years old.

The letters aroused my curiosity. They were addressed to my mother in an old-fashioned copperplate hand and opening one, I found a simple love letter written by a young man who was separated from his family by war. He was overjoyed by the birth of their baby girl. He had only seen his daughter once when she was just a few weeks old. He had been back to Ireland on leave granted following her birth and now he was missing his wife and newborn child. The years had faded the ink but I was still able to decipher the words.

My darling, he had written, *how much I miss you* ... As I read on, tears came to my eyes. Love poured off the pages and, for a few seconds, I believed it. He told her how he was in Belgium and, as a mechanic, he was placed at the rear of the advancing army.

No doubt surrounded by beautiful Flemish woman susceptible to his infectious smile and ready laugh, I thought sourly.

His closing sentences were: *I think how much Antoinette must have grown. It seems such a long time since I saw her. I count the days till I can hold you both again. Tell her that her daddy loves her and can't wait to see her again. Give her a big kiss from me.*

I looked down at the words written on thin paper all those years ago and grief threatened to overwhelm me – grief for what could have been, and for what *should* have been. An intense pain flooded my body. I staggered to the nearest chair as strength left me and slumped onto it. My hands rose to my head and gripped both sides of it as though by doing so I could fight the images that were forcing themselves in.

It was as though a projector in my head had sprung into life. A stream of unwanted pictures from the past flooded my mind: I saw Antoinette, the plump toddler, smiling up at her mother with the innocence of babyhood. I saw her just a few years later as the frightened child she had become after her father had taken away the essence of her childhood; he had stolen the innocence, the joy and the wonder and replaced it with nightmares. Sunny days had been denied her. Instead she had lived with fear and walked in grey shadows.

Why, I wondered over thirty years later.

A voice came into my head and spoke sternly to me: 'Stop looking for the actions of a normal man because he wasn't one. If you can't accept now what he was then, you never will accept it.'

I knew the voice spoke the truth. But memories that I had repressed resurfaced, cleared the protective mist from my mind and sent me back in time, to when one nightmare ended and another began.

I saw it as vividly as if it were yesterday: a girl, hardly old enough to be considered a teenager. I felt again her bewilderment, her despair and her feelings of betrayal. I saw her frightened and alone, not understanding why she had to suffer so much. I saw Antoinette, the victim.

Antoinette – the girl who used to be me.

Chapter Two

It was the day of her father's trial.

Sitting on a hard and uncomfortable bench outside the courtroom, Antoinette waited patiently to be called as the only witness in the case. Flanked on one side by the police sergeant and on the other by his wife, she sat without talking between the only two people who were offering her support.

She knew this was the day she had been dreading. Today her father was to be sentenced for his crime – the crime that would send him to prison. The police had made that very clear to her as they told her that he had pleaded guilty. Because of that, she would not be cross-examined but the court would want to know if she had been a willing participant in what had happened, or a victim of multiple rapes. The social workers had explained those facts to her. She was a week away from her fifteenth birthday – old enough to understand what they told her.

She sat silently, trying to escape her thoughts. She concentrated on remembering the happiest day of her childhood. It had been almost ten years previously, on another birthday in another life, before all the horror began, when her mother had given her a black-and-tan terrier puppy called Judy. She had loved Judy immediately and the little dog returned her affection.

Judy was at home right now, waiting for her. Antoinette tried to conjure up her pet's face and draw comfort from the one living creature that had always loved her, constantly and unconditionally. But try as she might, the image of the little dog faded, replaced by the memory of the day just after she'd turned six years old, when her father had first molested her.

Before long, he was abusing her three times a week, carefully when she was just a child and with more force as she grew older, though he helped her through it by giving her whiskey to numb her senses. Over the years it went on and she kept quiet, cowed by his violence and his threats that she would be taken away, reviled, disbelieved – blamed.

Then, when she was fourteen years old, she became pregnant. She would never forget the atmosphere of fear that hung over the house as she vomited every morning and her belly grew larger. Eventually, her mother, cold and uncaring, had told her to take herself to the doctor. It was the doctor who had told her she was expecting a baby. When he'd said, 'You must have had sex with somebody', she'd replied, 'Only with my father.'

There was an awful silence before he asked, 'Were you raped?'

She didn't even know what rape was. The doctor visited her mother and, between the two of them, they arranged for her to have a private abortion. It was all to be kept deadly quiet, for the sake of the family – but Antoinette had let someone else in to the secret. In her distress, she'd gone to a teacher's house and told her the truth. The teacher in turn had gone to social services. Then Antoinette and her father were arrested.

She had told the police everything, from that day when she was six and it had all started. She had also told them that her mother did not know about what had happened. She believed this because she needed to.

To an observer, Antoinette looked quite calm and composed as she waited to be called in to give her evidence to the court. She sat silently, alone apart from the police. Her mother had not come that day. She was neatly dressed in a grey skirt and her old school blazer which hung loosely on her slight frame. Her dark brown hair, styled in a page-boy cut, fell to her shoulders. She was an attractive teenager with a woman's body and a child's vulnerable face. Her pallor and the dark circles smudged under her eyes showed the sleepless nights she had endured and a slight tremor in her right eye revealed the stress that she was under – apart from that, she was expressionless.

The recent abortion of her father's child and the subsequent illness that followed had left her weak and exhausted. Shock and depression had given her an artificial calmness that appeared to others to be the composure of a child mature beyond her years.

Her emotions, too, were numb after her recent ordeal and, as she waited to be called, she felt very little. She knew that after the trial she would be going home to a mother who no longer loved her and a town who blamed her for everything she had suffered. Nevertheless, the years had taught her how to separate herself from her emotions and she remained outwardly calm.

Her wait ceased when the door of the courtroom swung open to allow the clerk of the court to walk briskly through. She knew that he had come to fetch her.

'Antoinette Maguire, the judge has a few questions for you.' He indicated that she should follow as he turned and walked back into the court.

The police sergeant and his wife smiled their encouragement but Antoinette did not notice. She concentrated on following the black-garbed clerk into the courtroom. Once inside, the silent pressure of the courtroom made her stop walking and, without looking, she could feel her father's eyes boring into her from the dock. Everything else around her appeared stern and forbidding: the dark sombre gowns of the barristers, the vivid scarlet formal robes of the judge, their wigs and their serious expressions.

She stood in the waiting courtroom, a small figure overwhelmed by her surroundings, with no idea what was expected of her. The formality of the court both bewildered and disoriented her as she waited for instructions. Then she felt someone touch her arm and show her where to stand. In a trance she stepped into the witness box where little more than the top of her head could be seen, as the judge spoke to her, telling her, as the clerk had said, that he had just a few questions to ask her. The clerk gave her the Bible and, in a voice that quivered, she repeated the oath.

'I promise to tell the truth, the whole truth and nothing but the truth, so help me God.'

'Antoinette,' said the judge, 'I just want you to answer a few questions, then you will be free to go. Just answer them to the best of your ability. And remember that you are not on trial here. Can you do that?'

She finally raised her eyes to meet the judge's, for the tone of his voice when he addressed her made her feel, that in some way, he was on her side. She kept her eyes focused on his. Then she could not see her father. 'Yes.'

The judge leant over, put his arms on the edge of his bench and looked at her in as kindly a way as he could. 'Did you at any time tell your mother about what was happening to you?'

'No.' She almost believed it to be true, for she had still blocked out the memory of when she had told her. She clenched her fists, digging her nails into the palms. She had thought that all her tears were dried up and she had nothing left to cry with but now they threatened to return. Her eyes prickled and stung but she used all her strength to hold them back. Nothing would let her cry in public and allow these strangers to see her shame.

'Do you know the facts of life? Do you know how women become pregnant?'

The atmosphere was tense as everyone waited for Antoinette's answer. She kept her eyes locked on the judge and tried to make the rest of the courtroom disappear as she whispered, 'Yes.'

She sensed her father watching her and felt the tension in the room increase as the judge asked the final question. She heard the intake of breath when it came.

'Then surely you must have been scared of becoming pregnant?'

It was a question she had been asked so many times, by social workers and the police and she told him exactly what she'd told them. She replied carefully, 'He used something. It looked like a balloon and he said that it would stop me having a baby.'

There was a collective sigh as everyone in the court breathed out. She had confirmed what they had all suspected, that Joe Maguire had calculatingly and systematically abused his daughter from the age of six and after she had matured to the point where she had her first period, he had worn condoms.

With Antoinette's answer, her father's defence disintegrated. He had tried to claim that his actions were those of a sick man who had been overcome by his impulses. His daughter's innocent description of a condom, something she did not even know the word for, gave the lie to this. His actions were not impulsive, they were premeditated. Joe Maguire was completely responsible for his actions.

The judge thanked her for her answers and told her she could leave the court. Still keeping her eyes averted to avoid her father's stare, she walked back alone through the double doors into the waiting area.

She was not present when the judge handed down her father's sentence. Her father's solicitor, paid for by her mother, gave Antoinette the details half an hour later.

Joe Maguire had received a four-year prison sentence for a crime he had committed over a period that had spanned seven years. He would walk free in thirty months; one third of the time that Antoinette had suffered.

She felt nothing. For a long time, the only way she had kept her sanity was by not feeling anything at all.

'Your father wants to see you,' continued the solicitor. 'He's in the holding cells.'

Still trained to obey, she went to see her father. The interview was short. He stared at her arrogantly, still secure in the knowledge that he could control her, and told her to look after her mother. Unable to break the habit of being a good daughter, she said she would. He showed no concern as to who would look after his daughter.

As she left the cells, she was told that the judge wished to see her in his chambers. There, with his wig and scarlet gown removed, he seemed less imposing and more kindly. Seated in the small room, she took comfort from his words.

'Antoinette, you will find, as I know you already have, that life is not fair. People will blame you, as they already have. But I want you to listen to me very carefully. I've seen the police reports. I've seen your medical reports. I know exactly what has happened to you, and I'm telling you that none of this was your fault. You have done nothing to be ashamed of.' He smiled and then walked with her to his door.

She left the court with his words tucked safely into her mind; words that over the years she would take out for comfort, words that helped her face a family and a town who did not share his opinion.

Chapter Three

I t was 1961 and Antoinette had just turned sixteen years old. Two years had passed since her father had been sentenced to prison for what the papers called 'a serious offence against a minor'. The trial had been held *in camera* in order to protect her identity but that hadn't mattered – the details were an open secret and everyone in Coleraine knew what had happened. They knew, and they blamed Antoinette. She had been a willing party, they whispered, or why had she kept quiet for so long? It was only when she got pregnant that she cried rape, and brought this terrible disgrace on her father's family.

Antoinette was expelled from school. Her father's family told her never to visit them again. The town shut its doors on her and shunned her wherever she went.

Ruth, Antoinette's mother, had been desperate to escape the disgrace of her husband's crime and prison sentence, and she wanted to get away as soon as she could from the gossip and whispers in the town. Nothing could have persuaded her to remain. The family house was hurriedly sold, as was Joe's black Jaguar car, but even after both sales had gone through, she had been left very short of money.

Undeterred, she moved herself and Antoinette from Coleraine to the poor district of the Shankhill Road in Belfast, and a small rented house. Antoinette, relieved that they had left Coleraine but with her dreams of an education in tatters, took jobs as an au pair so that she could help to contribute financially while Ruth got a position as the manageress of a coffee shop in the city.

But the fear pursued her. The terrible feelings of rejection by everyone she cared about would not release their grip on her. She felt lonely, unloved and worthless. The only solution, she thought, was to leave the world she no longer felt wanted by. It was then that Antoinette took pills, washed them down with whiskey and cut her wrists fifteen times with a razor. She survived, just, and spent three months in a mental hospital on the outskirts of Belfast. Because she was only fifteen, she was spared electric shock treatment and sedatives. Instead, intensive therapy helped to lift her depression and eventually she was well enough to leave and resume her life.

Ruth had managed to buy a home for them while Antoinette was ill, and it was to this new place that she went, feeling that perhaps her life might be about to improve for the first time in many years.

The gate lodge was a pretty Victorian building standing on the edge of the town. It had small, cramped rooms cluttered with cheap, shabby furniture; the plaster on the walls was old and lumpy and cracks of age ran across the window frames and marked the skirting boards. Curtains with large flowery prints designed for larger windows had been shortened and hung in ungainly folds half way down the walls while the clashing floral carpets were faded and threadbare.

'Here we are then, Antoinette,' said Ruth, as they went in for the first time. 'This is our new home. A room for you and a room for me. What do you think?'

From the first moment she went into the old house, Antoinette began to feel safe. She didn't know why this place should be where she began to leave the past behind, but it was. Here, the fear she had lived with for eight years, that had stalked her waking hours and invaded her dreams gradually diminished. Antoinette felt that the lodge was her nest, somewhere where she was protected from the world.

Together, she and her mother began to turn the place into their home. Bonded by their desire to create something homely and welcoming, they covered the bumpy old plaster with two coats of fresh paint, applied with amateurish enthusiasm. They made the tired old sitting room into a pretty individual room filled with books and ornaments. Ruth's collection of Staffordshire dogs were placed in one corner while willow-patterned plates were displayed on a scratched oak sideboard, alongside the little knick-knacks and pieces that Antoinette and her mother bought from Smithfield market in the centre of Belfast. It was there, among the stalls selling bric-a-brac and second-hand furniture, that they found their best bargains.

It was on one of those days when they went out exploring the market that Antoinette discovered a green wing armchair priced at two pounds. Full of excitement, she called her mother over to see it and together they quickly made the purchase. At home, it became Antoinette's favourite chair. She loved the soft velvet that covered it and the wings on the back that protected her from draughts.

As the weeks passed and they settled into their new home, the closeness with her mother that Antoinette had craved since she was six returned and the trust that she'd once had began to grow again. She cherished it so much that she never asked herself why everything that had gone before had happened; she firmly locked away the memories of how her mother had once been and refused to ask herself the questions that had haunted her. Instead, she looked to the future. At last she was in a place where she felt safe, and at last her relationship with her mother was beginning to blossom. She discovered that the satisfaction of being free to love far outweighed the happiness of receiving it. Like a flower in the sunshine, she began to bloom.

Ruth got Antoinette a job as a waitress in the coffee shop where she was the manageress. The work was not difficult and Antoinette enjoyed it. In the evenings, after they got home from work, she and her mother would eagerly scan the newspaper and choose from the two available channels a programme they both wanted to see. With their supper on a tray, they sat engrossed in old black-and-white films or quiz shows, kept warm by the coal fire burning away in the grate. The television was Antoinette's pride and joy – it was the only piece of furniture that had been bought new and she had saved the money to purchase it herself.

At the end of the evening, Antoinette would fill the hot-water bottles and carry them up the steep narrow staircase that led from the living room to a tiny square landing. On opposite sides of it, separated only by a few feet, were their unheated bedrooms with their sloping ceilings and ill-fitting windows. She would wrap each pink rubber bottle in a pair of pyjamas and tuck them into the cold beds to create a welcome patch of warmth for later.

Then, back downstairs, a final cup of hot chocolate would be drunk companionably before Ruth would depart, leaving

Antoinette to tidy up. Her last job was to damp down the fire with coal rubble and tea leaves so that in the morning, once prodded by the cast-iron poker that stood with its matching shovel and brush in the stand beside it, there would be a welcoming glow.

Antoinette would rise first in the morning and go downstairs for a quick sponge wash, taken hurriedly at the kitchen sink. The steam from the kettle would mingle with the mist of her breath as she boiled water for their morning tea. Once a week, a paraffin stove was lit. It gave off obnoxious fumes as well as a faint heat; while it warmed up, Antoinette dragged an old tin bath out and then filled it with saucepanfuls of boiling water. She would bath quickly and wash her hair, as the kitchen heated up; then, wrapped in a flannel dressing gown, she would clean the bath and refill it for her mother. Clothes were still washed by hand and hung on a line suspended between two metal poles in the small back garden. While still damp, they were aired in front of the fire causing steam to rise as the smell of drying washing filled the room.

On Sundays, when the coffee shop was shut, Antoinette would cook breakfast and she and her mother would share it together while Judy, now an old dog whose rheumatism was beginning to slow her down, would sit at Antoinette's side, her eyes following their every movement hoping that both mother and daughter were going to stay at home and not leave her. On the days that Ruth and her daughter left for work together she would follow them to the door, a look of abject misery which the years had perfected on her face.

It was a quiet life, but a comforting and healing one, as the great fissure that had once existed between Antoinette and her mother gradually began to close. The one thing they never talked about was what would happen on that distant day when her father was released. In fact, Ruth never spoke about her husband at all and there was never a letter from him in the house – not for Ruth the indignity of a letter marked with a prison stamp – and never one written to him, as far as Antoinette saw.

Her father's eventual release was a dark shadow on the horizon but that time was far off yet. There was no need to think of it now. Antoinette lived in blissful ignorance of Ruth's future plans. It was just the two of them now.

Eighteen months after they moved to the gate lodge, Antoinette resolved to do something about the ambitions that she had quietly been nurturing inside her. Although she liked her job at the coffee shop, she wanted more for herself than a life as a waitress, and she wanted to make her mother proud. But the problem was that prospective employers would be put off by the fact she had left school at sixteen with no qualifications. Without proof of her education, there was no way she could begin to better herself. But Antoinette had worked out a way to get around that. By going to a secretarial college, she would not only get a formal qualification but also a certificate that stated she had left school at eighteen, giving her those precious two extra years. All she needed was the money to pay the fees and she was already planning how that could be done.

She had heard that lots of Irish girls went over to England or Wales during the summer to work in the holiday camps. The pay was good and the tips were lucrative, she was told. It would be a quick and relatively easy way to earn the money she would need to put herself through college, and the coffee shop would let her take some time off to work elsewhere and then take her back when she returned. Belfast was always full of students looking for temporary work, so it wouldn't be hard to find someone to take her place for a while.

It felt wonderful to have a goal to work towards. When Antoinette explained her plan to the owner of the coffee shop, it seemed that fate was on her side. He had a relative who owned a hotel on the Isle of Man and who was always looking for staff. Why didn't she go out there over Easter and earn some good money as a combination of waitress and chamber maid? It seemed too good an opportunity to pass up and so within a fortnight Antoinette was on her way to the Isle of Man on the ferry.

It was not quite the enjoyable experience she had anticipated. The girls were treated as little more than glorified dogsbodies, kept on the run from the early hours of the morning till late at night. Antoinette found it exhausting and not as well paid as she had been led to expect. But with few opportunities and even less time for spending her money, her savings mounted up and she decided to come home a few days earlier than she'd originally planned and spend some time relaxing at the lodge before going back to work.

Excited to be returning home, she hurried back from the docks to Lisburn as fast as she could, wishing the taxi could go at twice the speed. But when she let herself into the lodge and dashed into the sitting room, her arms full of presents for her mother, she came to an abrupt halt, startled by the sight that she least wanted to see in the world.

'Hello. How's my wee girl?'

It was her father, sitting in the green wing armchair, smiling at her smugly, while her mother sat at his feet, her face alight with happiness.

Chapter Four

Antoinette lay in bed, unwilling to get up, trying to tell herself that the night before had just been a bad dream. But she knew it was real, hard though it was to accept it. She was incredulous – how could her mother have done such a thing? It was as extraordinary as it was cruel.

Unable to delay any longer, she pushed back the bedclothes, swung her legs to the floor and started to dress. Her whole body drooped as she pulled on clothes that had not changed in style since she had received her first pay packet. Her entire wardrobe consisted of pleated skirts and high-necked jumpers in muted hues; bland clothes that her mother liked. They were the uniform of a middle-class girl whose one wish was to conform and not to stand out from the crowd.

Antoinette waited in her bedroom until she heard her mother leave for work; she had no desire to confront her that morning and, besides, the hurt and anger were so great she hardly knew if she would be able to speak. Then Ruth called out, as she did every morning, 'I'm off to work now, darling. See you this evening!' Her voice was more cheerful than usual, no doubt because of her husband's weekend visit.

When she had heard the door slam behind her mother, Antoinette went downstairs. Judy was waiting at the foot of them and, as she had done so many times in the past, she sat on the floor and put her arms round the old dog's neck, resting her face against the warmth of the fur for comfort. Judy, sensing her despair, licked her face as though trying to offer consolation while Antoinette felt the tears come to her eyes then trickle silently down her cheeks.

She went into the living room. Her nostrils filled with the scent of an enemy – an enemy she had thought she would never have to face again. Like a small animal sensing danger, she stiffened.

She could smell him even in an empty room.

She knew then that she had not dreamt the events of the previous night. When she had seen her father sitting there, she'd been unable to speak. Instead, she'd fled the room, dropping her parcels, and taken sanctuary in her bedroom. There she had stayed until he had left, trying to understand what had happened and almost unable to believe her eyes. She had thought that she and her mother had started a new life together but now it seemed that Ruth had just been marking time until she could restart the old one. Antoinette had just been her companion while she waited.

Her father had left hours ago to return to prison when his weekend pass had expired yet that odour she remembered, of cigarettes and hair oil mingled with the faint smell of stale sweat, contaminated the room. Her eyes alighted on the ashtrays overflowing with the crumbled remains of her father's rolled-up cigarettes; here was the physical proof of his visit. She opened the windows, took the ashtray with its cigarette butts and emptied it, but his smell still lingered, unleashing unwanted memories.

Now she had to face up to the fact that her father's weekend pass, granted after he had served two years of his four-year

sentence, had brought him straight to his wife, who had
clearly been delighted to have him back. From what she had
seen, Antoinette knew that the visit had not just been toler-
ated by Ruth – it had been warmly welcomed.

Her father had been in her home, he'd tarnished it. She felt
as though she had suddenly stepped into quicksand and,
struggle as she might, she was being sucked down, back to the
past, back into that dark place she had been in for so many
years. She tried to hold on to the fragile strands of the safety
she'd known in the gate lodge, tried to push away the memory
of the previous night and draw comfort from her familiar
surroundings.

But, through the numbness of shock and disbelief, another
emotion was breaking through. The realization of her
mother's total betrayal started to fuel her anger, and gradually it consumed her.

'How could my mother still care for a man who has committed such a heinous crime? She knows what he did to me, her
own daughter. How can she still love him?' she asked herself
repeatedly, as she paced about the room. 'And if she has been
able to forgive him, then what can she really feel for me? Has
it all been a lie?'

Our hearts might belong to us but we have very little
control over where they go and Antoinette was no different;
one moment, she wanted to hate her mother and the next, she
longed to be comforted by her and have her love returned.

But she couldn't accept the answers to the questions she
asked herself. She felt ill at the thought that just a few feet
away from her bedroom, her parents had shared a bed again.

Had they had sex, she wondered. The idea that Ruth might
have done willingly what she had been forced to do made her
shudder. And worst of all, she knew that if her mother was

willing to have her father back in the house even for a moment, it meant that in a few months' time, when he was released, she would welcome him back for good into the home she shared with Antoinette.

The sense of security which she thought she had found disappeared; the bottom fell out of her world and she felt herself falling into an abyss of unbelieving despair. That morning the feelings of betrayal became firmly fixed in her mind and no amount of will-power could make them disappear ever again.

Chapter Five

During the weeks after her father's return to prison, a barrier of distrust replaced the warmth of friendship between Ruth and her daughter. There was an invisible wall between them, this time constructed by Antoinette. The betrayal she had felt when she saw her father sitting in their living room was too much for her to overcome and she wanted to get out and run away as far as she could, but she knew that was not an option open to her.

Now that she had amassed some savings to put towards her dream of secretarial college, Antoinette still wanted to follow her plan of working away for the summer despite her experience on the Isle of Man. Hundreds of Irish girls would leave their homes to work the summer season at the holiday camps, hotels and guest houses of the mainland. With accommodation and all meals provided, along with high wages and good tips from happy holidaymakers, they could return with a substantial sum of money.

She'd already got a job at Butlins lined up for the summer season and her father's date of permanent release, eighteen months earlier than the sentence handed down, was due before her departure. Could she bear staying at home after he had joined them there?

Up until now, she had not wanted to leave her mother, but faced with her perfidy and the prospect of having to share a house with her father, she longed to go. But if she left before she had earned enough money, she would use up her savings and have to say goodbye to funding further education. Without those all-important secretarial qualifications, she knew she was looking at a future of waitressing or shop work.

'What choice do I have?' she asked herself. She would be homeless. Nobody would rent a room to a girl who was under eighteen, even if she could have earned enough to support herself.

The money she could earn at the camp, though, added to what she had already saved, would pay for the secretarial course she so desperately wanted to take. With qualifications, she would be free to leave home, get her own flat in Belfast and be independent of her parents.

I'm frightened for my future, she told herself. I've seen too many middle-aged women trying to scrape a living by working long hours in second-rate restaurants, while the younger girls are given plenty of work at the better places where tips are high. Her jumbled thoughts scuttled around in her brain until she saw she had no option but to stay.

Every Saturday morning since Antoinette had lived at the gate lodge, she had seen the billowing white furls of the dance marquee being erected in an enterprising local farmer's fields. On a Saturday night, she had heard the beat of a band as the music floated in the evening air. She would lean out of her bedroom window as far as she could, straining to hear more while she looked longingly at the huge tent. Lit up by the many lights inside, it glowed against the dark of the sky, looking for all the world like a giant illuminated marshmallow.

She knew that in there, young people entered their own world where they had their own music, wore their own fashions and had fun. As she craned out of her bedroom window, she remembered what her mother had to say on the subject.

'Nice girls don't go to such places, dear. If a boy wants to take you out then he comes to the house and collects you properly. You certainly don't go looking for him in there.' Ruth would always add her strange humourless laugh to her pronouncement and smile her bright, empty smile.

Whenever her mother said this to her, Antoinette always replied obediently, 'No, Mummy', and was content to stay in with her mother, spending the evening pleasing Ruth by keeping her company.

Thing had changed now, though. Now she wanted to be part of that world she could see through her bedroom window. She wanted to go to the marquee. Weekends were going to become party time for her; she was going to mix with other teens and live as they did. She was certain that other girls' lives were not centred on their mothers but on fashion, make-up and weekend dances, and she wanted the same.

Antoinette looked at herself in the mirror, giving her reflection a cool, appraising look. She knew she was different. Even apart from her English accent, her clothes were old-fashioned and her dark brown hair, falling almost to her shoulders in a page-boy cut, was more suitable to a fourteen-year-old than a girl of seventeen. It was all down to Ruth's influence.

Not any more, thought Antoinette wistfully. I want to be like other girls. I'm going to be fashionable.

She thought of the groups of happy, confident young people she often served at the coffee bar when she worked the evening shift. The boys with their neatly cut hair, dressed in jackets and well-pressed trousers, might look like younger versions of their fathers but the girls had created their own style, one that looked as though it had very little to do with their mothers. Their hair was teased into the new fashionable beehive, and their faces were coated in a pale pan stick that contrasted harshly with their black-lined eyes which peered out at the world through thickly mascaraed lashes.

Antoinette's skin saw only a flick of powder, her lips wore a natural pink lipstick and her eyes were only enhanced by one coat of mascara. This set her apart from her contemporaries almost as much as her clothes did.

I'll start at once, she decided.

The glamorous, swinging sixties had begun and with them came a new affluence. Blue-collar workers became part of the middle classes and housing estates sprung up everywhere, offering young couples the chance to own their box-like house, identical to all the others nearby. Cars were parked outside every house, television aerials decorated every roof and the words 'hire purchase' replaced 'debt'. This was a boom time, and it brought with it a new youth culture that Antoinette longed to be a part of. Teenagers had found an assurance their parents had never known, and in their leisure time they danced to the new rock 'n' roll, went to cafés, drank cappuccinos and talked confidently together. They refused to be younger versions of their parents and instead invented their own fashions and attitudes.

These were the people Antoinette wanted to mix with and to do so she knew she would have to change. She could do little about her English accent but she could certainly change her appearance.

A very different Antoinette began to emerge. She bought tight dresses and hid them at the back of her wardrobe, along with stiletto-heeled shoes and new underwear. A hairdresser recommended by one of her youthful customers worked his magic and made the neatly cut dark brown hair disappear. In its place was a back-combed beehive. Plucked eyebrows now accented eyes that had grown harder, and a loss of appetite turned her once-plump shape into a more fashionable slim one.

Ruth watched the transformation, puzzled and displeased. She was used to unquestioning obedience from a child that had always sought approval, and she was taken by surprise by this sudden rebellion. While she did nothing to stop it, she fought back subtly, using her skill with words to manipulate her daughter and provoke the reaction she wanted. She used words full of hurt and bewildered anger for her emotional blackmail.

'I don't know why you want to make me unhappy. Don't you think I've suffered enough?' she would say plaintively.

But Antoinette refused to listen.

As the new, fashionable Antoinette took shape, she found that the girls who frequented the coffee shop now chatted to her. Her new friends' main interests were make-up, teenage fashion and how to get a boyfriend, and these interests took up most of their mental energy. Antoinette was grateful for this, as it left them with little curiosity about Antoinette's home life, so she didn't need to use the false one she had created: a happy home, a loving mother and a father who worked away.

The weekend when Antoinette decided she was going to complete her transformation arrived. The process took hours. First, a bright orange dye was washed through her hair and then she set about drying it and teasing it into that fashionable shape so loved by teenage girls and despaired of by their parents: it rose high above her hair, stiffened into place with a generous squirting of lacquer. It was so thickly coated that a comb could hardly penetrate it.

Then, her face. She took a pan stick and covered her skin with it so that she was strangely pale. She ringed her eyes so heavily in black liner that they appeared to have shrunk in size. Then she took up the latest addition to her fast-growing make up collection: a small plastic box complete with mirror containing a cake of black mascara. Generous gobbets of spit turned the black cake into a gooey mess which she carefully applied to her lashes. After each coat, she added another until the thickened lashes nearly weighed down the lids. Finally, the natural colour of her mouth was obliterated by the palest of gleaming pink lipstick studiously applied to puckered lips as she practised pouting in front of the mirror.

She looked at her reflection, pleased with what she saw. She pursed her lips and smiled. Much to her satisfaction, the mirror showed no sign of the shy studious teenager her mother knew, nor of the old-fashioned girl that worked at the coffee bar. No, this was a modern girl, one who shared the assurance of the people she admired.

She felt as though she had emerged from a cocoon, and had shed the safe skin of 'obedient daughter'. Deep down, she still lacked the confidence to be completely sure of the outcome of her metamorphosis but she tried to put that out of her mind.

Instead, she welcomed her new image. She pouted at the girl in the mirror.

'Goodbye, Antoinette,' she said. 'Hello, Toni.'

Her new self was born and she was a girl ready to party on a Saturday night.

Chapter Six

Now that Antoinette looked the part, the girls she'd met at the coffee bar invited her to share Saturday evenings with them. They would meet in groups and descend in a pack on the local dance venues, spending the evening dancing, giggling and flirting with the boys.

At last, Antoinette felt herself accepted. More than anything else, she wanted friends and the companionship of other young people. She needed desperately to be part of a group, to giggle companionably with them and to have what she had been missing her entire life: fun.

One Saturday morning, she excitedly watched the beginning of the conversion of the nearby field from muddy site into a magic place. At last she was finally going to enter that secret world, the one where teenagers dressed in the height of fashion, danced the night away, passed cigarettes around to appear sophisticated and drank smuggled-in alcohol. She couldn't wait.

She watched as coils of electric cables were run from large, noisy, diesel-fuelled generators to provide the sparkling lights that shone on the dancers. She saw a huge glitter ball, something she had only seen before on television, being carried into the tent.

Sections of wooden floors to be laid over the damp earth were taken in and then, once that was in place, the furniture followed. A small army of helpers carried in folding tables and an assortment of chairs was placed in groups around the hastily erected wooden dance floor. She had been told that there would be a bar inside, but that it only offered soft drinks. Anything stronger had to be smuggled in but that wasn't difficult. Customers with bulging pockets were given a cursory search by good-natured security guards as they looked for forbidden alcohol they seldom found. The walls of the marquee were easily raised and small bottles full of spirits slid under its folds to the eager hands of their co-conspirators.

Antoinette liked drinking. Ever since her father had first introduced her to the intoxication of spirits, she had enjoyed the sensation of numbness and relaxation that alcohol brought. While most teenagers were just discovering how to drink, Antoinette was a practised hand. Even now she liked to keep a bottle in her room so that she could take fortifying sips when she needed them. As soon as she had looked old enough, she had been able to buy it herself from off-licences, pretending it was for her mother.

At the moment, Antoinette had a small bottle of vodka, her chosen spirit, hidden in her room, in the belief that her breath would not be tainted by its smell. She did not know how easily available spirits were at the dances, so she decided to have some before she left, and poured herself a generous helping.

Fuelled by a double-vodka-induced confidence, she put on her American tan stockings, pinning them to her pink suspender belt. Then she slithered into a dress so tight that it nearly bound her knees together and forced her feet into high white stilettos. She teased her hair as high as it would go, then sprayed it with a coloured lacquer, turning it into a bright orange halo. As she applied her make-up, her face lost its glow and became deadly pale. Two black-rimmed eyes, more panda than doe-like, looked into the mirror one more time and she was delighted with what she saw. Now she was ready to hobble the short distance from the gate lodge to the marquee.

As she went downstairs and into the sitting room, Antoinette gave scant thought to what her mother's reaction would be when she was face to face with her daughter's transformation. But she heard the shocked intake of breath as she entered, and quickly averted her eyes from Ruth's horrified face as she made her way towards the front door. She didn't care what her mother thought. At last she was going to swing her tightly encased hips on the dance floor and that evening that was all that mattered to her.

For once Ruth was speechless and before she could regain her voice, Antoinette made her hasty exit.

'I'm off now!' she called unnecessarily as she closed the door firmly behind her.

A pack of girls, all dressed in similar attire to Antoinette, was waiting for her in the queue that had already formed outside the marquee. Once admitted, they made their way to the ladies' toilets where, giggling and chattering, they preened in front of the mirrors. Handbags snapped open for the teenage ritual of repairing make-up. They did not give a thought to the fact that a ten-minute walk from their homes to the tent was hardly likely to have disturbed their hours of work. Hair was once again tweaked and teased then sprayed liberally, filling the air with a cloud of cheap perfume. The tail end of a comb was inserted into the construction, lifting it even higher, and only then were they satisfied there was nothing more that could be done to it.

The girls carefully inspected their faces to make sure that enough make-up had been applied to mask their young complexions, and slicked on another coating of lipstick. Then, once content with the apparition in the mirror, the girls turned their attention to pinning, helping each other insert strategically placed safety pins into the long zipper of their dresses.

'Come on,' said one pert blue-eyed blonde to Antoinette. 'I'll fix you. Where are your pins?'

'I've not got any,' she replied. 'What are they for?'

There was a peal of girlish laughter at her naivety.

'Well, if you don't want to end up with your dress down to your waist, you have to pin. The boys will have been drinking at the pub and you know what that does,' said the girl, and she exchanged knowing smiles with her more experienced friends.

Until that moment, Antoinette had been completely unaware that zippers presented such irresistible temptation to the youths at the dance hall. She had only thought as far ahead as dancing and hadn't given any consideration to what the boys might expect. She gulped as a picture came into her mind of a horde of drunken youths with sweaty hands and 'one thing only on their minds'.

Sally, the blonde-haired girl who was the oldest in the group, saw the look of fear that had crossed her new friend's face.

'Don't look so scared,' she said, trying to reassure her. 'Most of the boys are just here for the crack. Oh, they won't say no to a chance but you'll be all right. Anyhow those pins put them off and stop their sweaty hands from climbing. I'll lend you a couple.'

Antoinette obediently turned round and Sally carefully inserted the safety pins on the inside of her dress, placing them along the zipper until the last one was pinned at the top of the dress. Once their dresses tugged back into shape, the girls made their way into the main part of the marquee where the band was already playing a fast number.

Antoinette found her feet were tapping to the music and felt her nervousness evaporate as she saw groups of youngsters all around her sitting, chatting or swinging their bodies on the dance floor.

The girls bought soft drinks and then talked nineteen to the dozen to each other while their eyes scanned every male present. The group took their seats. Boys dressed in sports jackets and trousers with firmly pressed centre creases walked in front of them before approaching to ask for a dance. When they were asked, the girls would look up, smile an acceptance and then, holding their dance partner's hand, allow him to lead her on to the dance floor.

Suddenly, Antoinette heard a voice ask, 'Would you like to dance?'

Looking up, she saw the smiling round face of a boy not much older than she was. She took his outstretched hand and did as she had seen her friends do, following him to the floor. She tried to remember the steps she had practised at home; then the rhythm of the band took over and she felt herself being swung into a jive.

It was a wonderful feeling and she was so happy that she remembered the moves of the new dances which she had only tried before in front of the mirror, with Judy as her only audience.

After the first dance, her partner requested a second and then a third. Then the band took a break and, buoyed up with confidence after her dances, she thanked her partner and rejoined her friends. Their group was a popular one, for they were vivacious girls out for a night of fun and their heavy make-up had not succeeded in masking their natural prettiness. Dance after dance was asked for, smuggled vodka spiked their drinks and Antoinette felt her confidence grow as, with flushed cheeks, she swung in time to the beat of the band.

Her first dance partner reclaimed her for the final dance. As the lights were dimmed, the slow music of the last waltz was the only sound she could hear. Alcohol made her body relax and she gave herself up to the pleasurable feel of being held, laying her head against his shoulder as they circled the floor. She raised her head while the music still played and felt a damp cheek with its light fuzz pressing against hers. Hands climbed uncertainly above her waist until they rested only a fraction below her breasts. Antoinette instinctively arched her back to avoid body contact. She removed one hand from around his shoulders as she covered his hand lightly, smiling as she gave a slight shake of her head. With that, she established that she liked him but was not easy.

She knew that if she wanted to be accepted by her group of new friends, she had to learn the games played by the sexes and the unspoken codes they communicated with.

Her dance partner was not ready to recognize defeat. Even with her hand still keeping his in place, he lowered his face to hers and she felt his lips searching for her mouth while the other hand tried in vain to mould her body to his.

Antoinette threw back her head, looked him in the eye and gave a light laugh while her body tensed against his manoeuvres. Seeing that she was a nice girl even if her appearance belied that fact, he slackened his hold and smiled back sheepishly. Boys of that age, as she was to learn, dreamt about finding easy girls but they very seldom succeeded.

Then the band played the last notes and the lights came on again. Happy and tired, Antoinette said goodbye to her girl-friends and returned home, the smell of cigarettes still cling-ing to her hair and the tang of alcohol still on her breath.

The smell lingered until the following morning when she came down to find her mother sitting in her armchair, wait-ing for her. She saw the look of disapproval on her mother's face as she recognized the familiar odour of stale alcohol and tobacco.

'Well, did you enjoy yourself last night?' asked Ruth, in tones that said she hoped for the contrary.

Her daughter, still wrapped in the glow of happiness from her first dance, refused to rise to the bait. 'Yes, thank you, Mummy,' she replied calmly.

'You know you looked a complete spectacle last night. Of course I can't stop you spending your money on what you like. But you're never to come out with me like that. I don't want to be embarrassed.' Ruth stood up and went to leave the room, but before she did, she delivered her parting shot. 'I don't know what your father will say about all this when he gets home.'

Too dazed by what she'd heard even to gasp, Antoinette stood staring after her mother. The pleasure from the night before drained away, replaced by a seed of panic. She never thought she would hear her mother say such a thing to her and it terrified her.

Over the next few weeks, the seed would take root, spread-ing until it invaded her dreams, making her nights restless as the panic rose, threatening to suffocate her.

Chapter Seven

Antoinette was soon going to dance halls every week. Soon, when she returned from the dances, another smell lingered on her breath: the smell of vomit. She had become unable to say no to another drink, even when the room was spinning and her stomach churned with nausea.

It became a familiar routine. As soon as she had hurriedly left the dance hall or marquee, the cold night air would hit her full face on but she had consumed too much alcohol for it to sober her. Instead, waves of queasiness would rise in her throat, making her gag. Holding a handkerchief to her mouth she would stagger to the shelter of the shadows cast by parked cars, hoping that she was hidden from view. Then, placing one hand on the boot of the nearest vehicle, she would try to keep her balance whilst, with eyes streaming, she would bend almost double as her body heaved with the effort of rejecting the alcohol. Hot bile would spurt out of her mouth, burning her throat as it did so until she felt there was nothing left inside her.

Then depression, the natural successor of alcohol-fuelled elation, would always swamp her as she wiped her mouth with a scrap of handkerchief, straightened up and resumed her wobbly walk home.

Her experience of alcohol when she was younger had shown her that it could help to dull mental anguish as well as physical pain. But she did not realize that she had crossed the narrow boundary that lay between a drink-fuelled party girl and an alcohol-dependent teenager. Even if she had realized that she had a problem, she would not have cared. All she knew was that with each sip she took, the better she felt: her fear receded, her misery disappeared and her confidence grew. She could tell stories that made people laugh, feel she was accepted as part of a group and, once in bed, escape her thoughts in a drink-induced stupor.

But there was a price to pay. On Sunday mornings, she wakened reluctantly, unwilling to face the results of the previous night's excesses. Her head pounded. From behind her eyes and across her head, waves of pain shot into her skull. Her tongue felt swollen, her throat dry, and all she wanted to do was stay under the bedclothes for the remainder of the day. But she refused to give her mother satisfaction by giving in to her self-inflicted misery; she knew that Ruth already thought she had enough reason to complain about her daughter's behaviour without Antoinette giving her fresh ammunition.

Instead, she tried to recall the night before. She would see the dance hall where groups of girls sat chattering and giggling as they studiously avoided the looks from groups of boys walking around them. Antoinette was beginning to understand how the game worked now. This was a competition between Antoinette and her friends of who could look the most nonchalant and the prize was to be asked to dance by the boy they'd already selected. As he approached, a blank look would replace the animated expression shown to her friends and coolly, almost reluctantly, she would accept his invitation to dance with a stiff nod of her beehived head.

Both sexes knew what they wanted: the girl wanted to be pursued and courted and then to win a steady boyfriend. The boy wanted to show his friends he could have any girl he wanted.

But for all their bravado, the boys knew the rules. They might try to get further but there was no surprise when they couldn't. They knew that a passionate kiss in the back of a car and a quick fumble would only lead to a soft but firm hand holding him back. In the early sixties, before the birth pill had led a sexual revolution, a pregnancy would result in either marriage or disgrace; both sexes knew that, and for different reasons, wanted to avoid them.

Antoinette, though, was playing a different game. She wanted vodka. She longed for her world to blur; she embraced the dizziness, then ran her wrists under the cold tap and splashed water on her pulse points to steady herself before looking for a refill. She smiled sweetly at the nearest boy whom she knew had a smuggled bottle. Mistaking her motives, he would hastily top up her glass and when she knew that no more would be forthcoming unless she parted with more than a smile, she would drain the glass and make a rapid departure.

Not for Antoinette a hasty grope in the back of a car, or the struggle to maintain her modesty as some youth, looking for a return on the free drinks he had given, tried to hoist her skirt up. She had no interest in that particular barter system and always made her escape before it could begin. Her friends were too young to be aware that drink not boys had become her obsession. But Ruth knew only too well.

It was drink that stopped her facing the fact that every-thing between them had changed. The trust and friendship that was so important to her had now slid away. Ruth had finally shown her plans to her daughter and Antoinette felt that any chance of survival was to exorcise that love that still remained.

Antoinette knew that her mother had begun to see her daughter as a problem, just as she had during those terrible years when she had refused to acknowledge what was happening. Now, as Antoinette slipped away from her control, Ruth obviously thought of her daughter as yet another burden she had to bear in a life strewn with unfulfilled expectations. Antoinette sensed that Ruth had begun to believe that her daughter was the cause of her problems.

Now she had made it clear that she would welcome her husband back into their home as though nothing had ever happened, she began to undermine Antoinette as much as she could, bullying her with subtle and skilful manipulation until she forced her daughter to accept the situation.

Ruth wanted control and she knew very well the words that would always make her daughter dance to her tune.

'You are such a worry to me, dear,' she would begin. 'I can't get to sleep until you come home. That's why I'm so tired in the mornings. Do you really want to worry me so?'

When she tired of making Antoinette feel guilty, there were her attacks – 'You're such a disappointment to me' – and her accusations – 'I don't know who you're with or what you and your friends get up to at those places but I know what you smell like when you come home.'

Antoinette tried to ignore her as she defiantly watched *Juke Box Jury* and, with a mirror propped in front of the television, applied make-up ready for another big night out. Then Ruth would play her ace.

'You know I love you.'

Antoinette longed for it to be true; underneath the anger she felt at her mother's betrayal, she still loved her and craved to be loved in return. Over the weeks that fell between that visit and her father's release, she tried to shut out the sound of her mother's voice as Ruth tried to seek her compliance in rewriting history. Her mother jerked the strings harder over the next few weeks until obedience, that integral habit of her daughter's childhood, started to win out. She demanded that Antoinette play the game of happy families, that she pretend that she was looking forward to her father's return and that nothing had ever happened that might make the very idea monstrous to her.

'Daddy will be home soon, dear,' Ruth would say to her daughter, her voice happy and untroubled, as though she expected nothing less than a delighted response.

Antoinette would feel her stomach clench, her fists tighten and the fear rise, but she said nothing.

Ruth would say in sharp tones that forbade any argument, 'I want you to try not to upset him, dear.' Then add in the patient voice of the martyr she seemed to believe she was, 'I've suffered enough! Nobody knows how much I've suffered. I can't take any more.'

Antoinette believed in her mother's suffering – she had heard that refrain 'I've suffered enough!' so often that she had to – but she didn't see it in her mother's eyes. Instead, she saw in Ruth anger at being thwarted, coldness and an implacable need to cling on to her own version of reality.

The day her father was expected home loomed on the horizon. For years, she had tried to block the date of his release from her mind but now it was impossible. The image of his face and the derisory tone of his voice haunted her sober hours – hours that were becoming fewer and fewer.

The week before his arrival Ruth triumphantly produced a packet containing a brown hair rinse.

'That red beehive has to go. If you want to do your hair like that when you are with your friends I can't stop you, but while you live here you are going to leave the house looking decent,' she told her daughter firmly.

Antoinette knew better than to protest. Having her mother furious with her a few days before her father was due home was not, she knew, a good idea. Sighing, she took the rinse, brushed her hair until it was straight and then applied the dye. One hour later, when she had given her hair its final rinse, then towel-dried it vigorously in front of the fire, she looked in the mirror and was faced with the reflection of a drab Antoinette. Of Toni, who, with all her mistakes, had courage, there was no sign. In her place was a frightened teenager that looked like the victim she had once been.

Her mother had won – she had destroyed the confidence that Antoinette had managed to build up since her father had vanished from their lives. And now, as his return loomed, she felt more than ever that she was being sent back to the place she had started out from.

Her mother looked at the new hair colour. 'Very nice, dear,' was her only comment, said without warmth. It was not meant as a compliment.

The night before her father was due to arrive an uneasy silence hung between Antoinette and her mother. Antoinette just wanted to escape to her room and block the thoughts of her father and his arrival from her mind, while Ruth was determined that the charade of a happy family would be played out in full.

When her mother was silent, Antoinette knew that it was only the prelude of worse to come and as the evening wore on, her nervousness increased.

'Well, I think I'll go to bed now,' she said eventually. 'I'm feeling very tired tonight.'

It was then, knowing she had won and that her daughter's short-lived rebellion was firmly under control, that Ruth delivered her *coup de grâce*.

She looked up at her daughter and said, 'Tomorrow, dear, I want you to meet Daddy and bring him home. I have to work in the morning and I know you are on the evening shift so you have the day free.' Opening her purse, she drew out a ten-shilling note and thrust it into her daughter's hand, giving a smile that showed more steely determination than sincerity. Then, as though she had planned a special treat, she said, 'Here's some money so you can buy him afternoon tea at that coffee shop you like so much.'

Stunned into obedience, she said, 'All right, Mummy.'

As she spoke, Antoinette felt her mother's power over her slip back into place and saw the gleam of satisfaction in Ruth's eyes as she smelt victory. As she had done every night before her brief rebellion, Antoinette kissed her mother quickly on the cheek and went to bed.

She knew in her heart that she had been successfully sucked through the looking glass into her mother's fantasy. She understood somehow that her mother needed to believe that she, Ruth, was a good wife and mother and that Joe was the handsome Irish husband who adored her. Between them, they had a daughter who was nothing but trouble and Ruth suffered because of it. She had been the victim of her husband's disgrace, but as long as Antoinette behaved herself and did not annoy her father when he came home, everything would be all right.

In Ruth's universe, Antoinette was the difficult daughter who had caused all the problems. Although she tried to fight it, it would not be long before Antoinette began to believe that perhaps her mother was right.

Chapter Eight

The coffee shop where Ruth had arranged for Antoinette to meet her father was one of the many that were rapidly springing up in the centre of Belfast. These forerunners of wine bars sold cappuccino coffee to the youth of Belfast and this one was Antoinette's favourite. It was there that she and her friends met before going to the dance halls, where they would sip their frothy drinks as they made plans for the evening ahead.

That afternoon, on the day of her father's release, she felt no pleasure in the familiar surroundings; the darkness of the interior looked gloomy to her while the large silver and black coffee machine, usually alive with a friendly hissing and gurgling, stood silently on the bar.

It was too early in the day for the hordes of people who frequented it in the evening to be present, while the lunchtime crowd, a mixture of smartly dressed businessmen and sophisticated women, had returned to their offices.

Her father's imminent return had sunk Antoinette into a depression. It was like a black hole that she had sunk into, where she could not even think about tomorrow. Even the simplest task seemed impossible and anything was liable to make her panic. All her responses shut down and she became the robot she had once been, secure only when obeying orders.

And then there were her other worries. What could she say if she met one of her friends? How could she explain him away? Why had her mother arranged for them to meet on what Antoinette saw as her territory? It was as though any independence that she had gained, any life that she had forged out for herself, had been taken away from her.

All those thoughts were running through her head as she walked to one of the wooden tables and took a seat. His bus was due to arrive at 3 p.m. She was grateful for this as she knew that the chances of bumping into anyone at that time of day were slim.

Which father was going to greet her, she wondered. Would it be the 'nice' one, who eleven years ago had met his wife and daughter at the Belfast docks; the father who had made Ruth glow with happiness as he hugged her and made his daughter giggle with pleasure when he swung her five-year-old body in the air, and then kissed her soundly on both cheeks? That father, the jovial man who had chucked her under the chin as he presented his wife with presents of boxes of chocolates after one of their many rows, was now only a dim memory. Or would it be the other father, the one with the bloodshot eyes and the mouth that quivered with rage at the very sight of her? Her childhood fear of the man she remembered most vividly, the one she had tried to force out of her mind, came back to her.

Antoinette arrived early. She was dressed as her old self: her newly washed hair now hung to the collar of her navy jacket and a grey skirt and pale-blue twin set had replaced the teenage uniform of jeans and shirt. Her mother had come into her room early that morning. She had made preparations to see her husband again and was dressed in a grey jacket with a fur collar that framed her face, softening it. Her hair was freshly permed with a copper rinse to hide the grey that had appeared in recent years and once again fell in soft waves about her face. Her mouth was painted a bright red, a colour she had always favoured, while rings sparkled against the hands tipped with scarlet-lacquered nails. She had opened the wardrobe and selected the clothes she wanted Antoinette to wear.

'That looks so nice on you, dear,' she had said. 'Wear that today.'

'I don't like it,' Antoinette had muttered. 'It's old-fashioned.'

'Oh no, dear, it makes you look very pretty. It's your colour blue. Wear it to please me, won't you?'

And she had.

Antoinette wanted to arrive before her father so that she had the advantage of being seated at a table with a clear view of the door. She wanted to see him before he saw her.

Hanging lamps cast soft pools of warm light on the wooden tables. A cup of coffee had been brought to her and she needed both hands to hold it to her mouth because her palms were damp and slippery with the moisture that fear brings. Her stomach fluttered with nervous tremors and her head felt light from a sleepless night.

She felt his presence a split second before she saw him. Looking up at the door, she could only make out a male form. With his back to the sun, he was a faceless shadow but she knew it was him. She felt the short hair on the back of her neck bristle and she placed her hands on her knees to hide the shaking.

It was not until he reached her side that his features came into focus.

'Hello, Antoinette,' he said.

As she looked into his face, she saw someone she had not seen before: the remorseful father. He'd been in prison for over two years and apart from that weekend leave, when she'd only seen him for a few moments, she had not spoken to him.

'Hello, Daddy,' she replied. Not wanting to hear any words from him she blurted out, 'Mummy's given me some money to pay for your tea.'

Such was Antoinette's conditioning to behave normally, she did. To any outsider the two of them presented a perfectly ordinary spectacle – a man taking his daughter out to tea.

The moment she said her first words to her father, Antoinette took another step further into her mother's world. It was a world where her sense of self-will disappeared, where she danced to the tune that Ruth sang. She had no choice, she had to comply. She acted her part in the charade that everything between them all was normal.

But it was far from normal. This was a man who had been sent to prison, and it was her evidence that had placed him there instead of in the psychiatric ward that her mother had hoped for, the lesser of two evils. She had wondered ever since what his reaction to her would be when they faced each other again and now she was about to find out.

She forced herself to hide her fear and look at him. She expected to see changes, even infinitesimal ones, in a man who had been incarcerated for a sexual crime. Even though the papers had not stated that the minor he was reported to have abused was his own daughter, the fact that his victim was an underage girl should have had some effect. Surely the other prisoners would have shown disapproval. Surely his popularity with other men would have disappeared. Surely not even his skill with a snooker cue could have saved him.

But to Antoinette's mystification, he looked no different than he had on the day of his trial. His tweed suit, which he had worn then, still fitted him perfectly; his tie was knotted firmly under the collar of his smoothly ironed pale-blue cotton shirt. His hair, with its auburn lights glinting in its thick waves, looked freshly barbered and his eyes reflected not a care in the world as they returned her gaze with a warm smile.

He took the seat opposite her and leant forward and placed his hand lightly over hers. She felt her fingers stiffen as they recoiled from his touch, then felt them tremble. She wanted nothing more than to rise from her seat and run. She didn't even have the strength to avoid meeting his hypnotic stare.

'I'm sorry,' he said, as though those words carried a magic formula that would make his deeds disappear in as many seconds as it took to utter them.

But she wanted desperately to believe in him. She wanted to have her faith in the adult world restored, and to enter a time machine where those awful years could be rewritten. Most of all, she wanted to be a normal teenager with two loving parents and a happy childhood, laden with memories that she could take with her to adulthood. She wanted to be able to smile at her recollections of the past, to be able to share them with her friends. She knew that the stories of our past, our families and of our friends create the structure of life but hers were too terrible to recall, let alone to tell other people.

She looked at the remorseful father and wanted to believe him – but she didn't.

Joe believed he had won. He smiled and ordered tea and scones. Antoinette watched him wash down his food with cups of tea but she was unable to eat. She just stared blankly at him and felt the familiar fear return. When she was little, it would make her glassy-eyed with terror while sickness swirled in her stomach.

Eventually he put down his cup and smiled at her. 'Well, my girl, if you've finished we might as well make a move.' He made no comment at her lack of appetite, just told her to call for the bill and settle it. Then he took her arm in imitation of a caring father and held it firmly as he led her from the café.

Antoinette and her father sat side by side on the bus that took them on their short journey from the centre of Belfast to Lisburn where the gate lodge was. They had taken seats upstairs so that he could smoke. She watched him roll a cigarette, saw the tip of his tongue slowly moisten the paper before he lit it, then felt him relax as he contentedly blew curls of smoke into the air.

She breathed in the fumes, letting them mask the familiar smell of his body that had always repelled her. She tried to make herself as small as possible. His arm pressed against hers and the heat from his body scorched her side at the point of contact. She turned and looked out of the window. His reflection was staring back at hers and on his mouth he wore a smile of insincere warmth, the one she remembered from her childhood.

When they arrived at their destination, Joe and his daughter alighted almost in tandem. He held his small suitcase in one hand and her elbow with the other. She tried not to flinch as the pressure of his fingers on her arm left her with no choice but to walk swiftly by his side. With every step, she felt an overwhelming desire to shake his hand off but the years of having her thoughts controlled had stripped away her will power and she could do nothing.

Once inside the small hallway, he dropped his case on the floor. Judy appeared to greet Antoinette and, seeing her, Joe dropped down and ran his fingers roughly over the little dog's head as a way of greeting. Judy didn't respond with the rapturous welcome that he felt was his due, so Joe pulled her ears and forced her face towards him. Unused to such rough treatment, Judy wriggled to escape and then crept to her mistress's side. She hid behind Antoinette's legs and gave a suspicious look at the interloper.

Annoyance flashed across his face. Even dogs had to like Joe Maguire.

'Judy, do you not remember me?' he asked in a jovial tone that barely covered his displeasure.

'She's old now, Daddy,' said Antoinette quickly, hoping that would shield her pet from his irritation.

He seemed to accept the excuse. He walked into the small living room, sat on the most comfortable chair and surveyed both her and his surroundings with a satisfied smirk.

'Well, Antoinette, aren't you pleased to have your old man home?' His voice was laden with mockery. Taking her silence as acquiescence, he said, 'Make me a cup of tea like a good girl, then.' Almost as an afterthought he pointed to the case carelessly dropped by the door. 'First take that up to your mammy's and my room.'

As she stooped to lift it, she saw through lowered eyelids a smug smile cross his face. He knew now that two years of absence had not undone the years of training that had suppressed her normal emotional growth. Antoinette was no rebellious teenager – he had seen to that.

She saw the smile and understood it. She picked the case up without a word. His authority remained unbroken and she was aware of it, but she knew she had to conceal the resentment that was rising in her. As she took the case and went back to the stairs, she could feel him watching her every move.

She dumped the case inside the door of her parent's room, trying not to look at the bed she knew he would now share with her mother. Then she went back down to the kitchen where, robot-like, she filled the kettle and placed it on the hob. Memories of other occasions, when she had used that ritual of tea making as a delaying tactic, sprang into her mind.

It was her mother who came to mind. Inwardly, Antoinette railed at her and asked the questions she was longing to hear the answer to. 'Mummy, how can you put me in danger like this? Don't you love me at all? Don't those years with just the two of us mean anything to you at all?'

But she knew the answers to those questions now.

The whistle of the kettle interrupted her thoughts as she poured boiling water over the tea leaves. Remembering her father's temper if he was kept waiting, she hastily set a small tray with two cups, poured milk into a jug and placed the sugar bowl beside it, before carefully carrying it through to him. She placed it on the coffee table, and then proceeded to pour out the tea, remembering to put the milk in first, and then two teaspoons of sugar, exactly as her father liked it.

'Well, you still make a good cup of tea, Antoinette. Now tell me, have you been missing your old man then?'

She flinched as she recalled the many times he had tormented her with similar questions, questions that she could never answer correctly and that eroded her confidence and confused her.

Before she could answer, a loud knock on the front door started Judy barking and pulled Antoinette out of her misery.

Her father made no effort to leave the comfort of his chair, clearly expecting her to answer it.

Grateful that she had been saved from replying, she went to the door and opened it to find herself facing a slightly built man in his middle years. His sparse sandy-coloured hair was parted at the right side and his light grey eyes, framed in gold-rimmed glasses, showed no spark of warmth. His dark suit was partly obscured by a three-quarter-length cream gabardine mackintosh but she could see his striped tie knotted with precision under the collar of his gleaming white shirt.

She had never seen him before and, being unused to strangers calling at the house, gave him an uncertain smile and waited for him to state his business. She received a cool stare that looked her up and down and, in response to her curious expression his hand flipped open a slim wallet. He held it in front of her eyes to show the identity card inside then finally spoke.

'Hello,' he said in a cold tone. 'I'm from social services. Are you Antoinette?'

Again that name she hated. That name with its associated memories was the name of someone she no longer wanted to be. A name that had hardly been heard since her father had gone to prison was now constantly repeated on the day of his release. Every time she heard it she felt the identity of 'Toni' slip further away. Hearing her name on her father's tongue was making her regress into that frightened fourteen year old she had been when he left. Now this stranger was using it. She felt a sense of foreboding as she looked at him uncomprehendingly. Why would social services call now, she wondered. They had done very little to help her before.

'May I come in?' he asked. The words might have been couched as a question but his attitude turned them into a command. 'I have to speak to you and your father.'

She nodded and stood aside to allow him to walk through the door into the sitting room. The social worker glanced at what he saw as a cosy scene with evident distaste. Antoinette recognized his reaction and was instantly aware of his aversion to her but her ingrained politeness made her offer him tea, which he disdainfully refused.

This man had not come to help her, she knew, but had already passed judgement and found her guilty, of what she did not know.

She sat on a hard-backed chair, clasping her hands together in her lap to control the slight shake that always betrayed her nervousness, as the visitor seated himself on the only other comfortable chair. He carefully hitched his trousers at the knee to protect their creases, allowing a glimpse of pale ankles to show above his socks, as he did so. Antoinette noticed that his fussy manoeuvre did not prevent his bony knees making little sharp points against the fabric. His feet, neatly placed together, were encased in black shoes so shiny she wondered if he could see his face in them when he bent to tie his laces.

His pasty face, with its nondescript features, turned to her father as he made pleasant small talk to Joe while ignoring her. He seemed on the surface a harmless little man but there was something about him – the coldness of his eyes, his fastidious appearance, the finicky way he opened his briefcase and placed a paper on his lap – that made her twitch with apprehension. She knew that his eyes might be turned to her father, but in the moments they had alighted on her, they had assessed her and found her lacking.

It only took a few minutes for Antoinette to understand the reason he had come to the house. He turned the conversation to the purpose of his visit: he wanted to know what plans Joe had made for the future. He was a recently released prisoner and, after all, prisons were meant to rehabilitate. A conscientious social worker's responsibility was to ensure that sufficient help was given on the outside to follow that principle through.

'So, Joe, have you any job interviews lined up?' he asked.

Joe said that yes, his interviews with the local army offices were already arranged – they were hiring good mechanics from the civilian sector. With his old references and the fact he had volunteered for active service during the war, Joe was confident he would be offered work.

All the time Antoinette knew, by the covert glances that were thrown surreptitiously at her, that somehow she was another reason social services had called.

Seemingly satisfied with Joe's answer, the social worker looked sternly at her, although he aimed his next remark at both of them.

'You are to behave yourselves, do you hear me?'

Antoinette saw the flicker of her father's temper in his eyes, and saw him quickly hide it.

'Yes,' he muttered. He realized that something more was expected of him and he flashed the social worker his charming smile and said in a rueful tone, 'I've learnt my lesson and all I want to do now is make it up with my wife. She's not had it easy while I've been away and I want to make amends.'

'Well, Joe, stay off the drink, won't you?'

To Antoinette's amazement, her father rose from the chair, crossed the few feet that separated him from the visitor, stretched out his hand and clasped the man's hand. 'Oh, I will, don't you worry,' he said, and again his smile appeared.

Feeling his duty was done, the visitor rose from his chair, clutched his briefcase and prepared to leave. Then he turned to Antoinette, fixed her with a look of disdain and said, 'And you, Antoinette, you're to be good, do you hear me?'

Seeing he was waiting for her reply, she stuttered, 'Yes.'

Satisfied with her mortification, he walked towards the door. She followed him into the hall to see him out and, as the front door closed behind him, she felt the last scraps of her hard-won new self-confidence disappear. The two years since her father had been sent to prison fell away and once again she was the teenager of fourteen who had been both blamed and shunned because of her father's crime.

As she heard the social worker's footsteps retreat, she lent against the hall wall and tried to regain her composure before she faced her father. She made herself recall the judge's words that day in his chambers: 'People will blame you ... and I'm telling you that none of this was your fault.' But she had always been besmirched by the dirt of other people's opinions and today the judge's words had lost their power to comfort her.

She felt that, yet again, she was at the mercy of the adult world and that it had betrayed her again, just as it had when her father's crime had come to light.

She went back to the sitting room, wondering what mood the social worker's visit might have put her father in. He showed no reaction to the unwanted caller but held his cup out for a refill. Then he said, 'Don't be talking about that man to your mother, Antoinette. She's had enough worries.'

To press his point home, he gave her an intimidating glare, and then resumed slurping his tea. The visit was never mentioned again.

Chapter Nine

The past receded and I was back in the sitting room of my father's house.

I blinked my eyes shut against those memories from a different era but still felt the depression left by Antoinette's ghost.

She had felt so unloved and that fact alone made her feel worthless; vulnerable people, lacking in confidence, see themselves through other's eyes.

One thought played on her mind: if my parents love me so little, some part of me must be to blame.

Whatever the mirror showed her, it was not what she saw; instead of an attractive teenager, she saw an ugly one. Instead of a victim, she saw a guilty party. Instead of a likeable girl, she saw someone who deserved rejection.

Why had she not protested, then? Why had she simply not packed her bags and gone? As an adult I knew the answer. Intense grief debilitates the mind so strongly that it is temporarily paralysed. Stripped of free thought, the mind is then incapable of making even the simplest decisions, far less planning an escape. Antoinette was simply frozen with despair.

If only she had been capable of walking away and never seeing them again, but she was not yet seventeen in an era when teenagers did not leave home to live in shared flats. She had only felt safe over short periods of her life and tiptoed round her parents shackled with a lead weight of dread at the thought of displeasing them. But however unhappy she felt her home life was, the unknown frightened her more.

She believed she needed whatever remnants of normality that being part of a family gave. None of the girls she knew lived away from home and at that stage not only did she want to blend in with her peers, she still had plans for her future. She hoped that if her father was working and contributed to the household, then surely Ruth would not be so dependent on her income.

Antoinette thought if that responsibility was lifted from her shoulders, then she could take her secretarial course. The three months working away in Wales at Butlins for the summer season would add to what she had already accumulated in the post office. That would cover her for a year while she took the course and once qualified she would be free to leave home forever.

Remembering the past, I pictured her agonizing over her future.

My adult hands shook with the desire to knock on the window of that gate lodge. I wanted to travel back through the years to protect her and change the direction of where Antoinette's confused thinking was taking her. My mind walked through the door and I was in the room standing next to her; the decades fell away as the adult and the teenager I had once been shared the past.

I looked into her eyes, haunted now, as she felt the home she had loved entrap her and her choices narrow. And through the chasm of years that separated us I tried to make her hear me.

'Don't stay!' I pleaded silently. 'Listen to me! Leave now! While your mother's at work, pack your case and go! You don't know what will happen if you stay, but I do.

Put your education off; pick it up when you are older. If you stay they will destroy you, Antoinette. Your mother will never protect you. Believe me, there is worse to come.'

Antoinette bent to fondle her dog's ears. She had failed to hear the voice of her future. I heard the ticking of the mantle clock as it moved relentlessly forward. Clocks very seldom move backwards and, knowing that, I wept for her.

Again I saw the picture in my mind of Antoinette being sent to meet her father. I felt her struggle for survival as she clung on desperately to her individuality. She refused to be completely controlled by her parents and I heard, again, the uncouth tone of her father's voice as he constantly belittled her attempts.

I felt a rueful smile cross my face as I pictured those dances that had the innocence of another time. I remembered with nostalgia the emerging youth culture that my generation was part of and then felt sadness at the thought of the teenager I had once been trying to establish a normal life.

And once again I felt her loneliness.

She had invented a new persona to hide behind: the party girl who had fooled her friends, but not herself. All the time she hid her fear that she would be asked questions about her family life and her past. If that happened, she was sure to be unmasked as a fraud. They were fears that no normal teenager should have had. She had turned to drink, embracing it as a friend that could allay her worries, then, when it had turned into her enemy, fought a battle to banish its power over her.

My attack of depression was replaced by a burst of anger at two people who had destroyed the childhood of a third.

I drew deeply on a cigarette, angrily flicked ash on the growing mound of butts that was now piled in the ashtray and then another thought entered my mind.

My father was dead. He was not going to return to his house. In the desk I had found that wallet with his emergency fund. A smile crossed my face as an idea entered my mind. What good use could I put it to? Now what did he hate spending money on? Meals out was certainly one. I remembered how much my mother had enjoyed going to a smart restaurant and how he had given a derisory snort at what he said was a total waste of his hard-earned cash.

'Well, today he can pay for one!' I exclaimed. I picked up the phone to dial my friend's mobile. She had come with me to Ireland to help support me as I confronted my father's death and dealt with the arrangements for his funeral, and was staying at a hotel nearby. As I called her, I searched my memory for other sacrileges which would have driven my father to fury. Any woman driving his gleaming red car which was parked outside would certainly have outraged him. So we'll go in that, I thought with glee.

When my friend answered her mobile, I said, 'How do you fancy going out to lunch? Somewhere nice and expensive. It's on me. I'll collect you in twenty minutes.'

Then I called my insurance broker in London to arrange cover on the car and the last call was to the restaurant to make a booking for two. Then, picking up the keys of my father's car which had been conveniently left on top of the desk, I strode out of the house, inserted the keys triumphantly in the ignition, turned the radio on to full blast and drove off.

After I'd collected my friend, we cruised slowly along the windy coast road that leads to the Giants Causeway. Unlike so much of England, the landscape of Ireland had not altered much since I had first arrived there as a small child. There weren't acres of new houses or high-rise flats. Instead, it was as beautiful as ever. As we drove along the coastal road, a breathtaking scenery of green hills stretched away to our left, while miles of unspoilt beaches lay on our right. There I could see a few warmly wrapped figures walking in the bracing air from the Atlantic Ocean, while greedy seagulls, in their ever-lasting quest for food, swooped overhead.

I opened my window to smell the salty air and to hear the crash of the waves as they met the shore. This was the Ireland that I enjoyed, a country that without my past, I could have felt part of.

We drove through tiny hamlets with their small, squat, single-storey houses lining the streets. Instead of the raggedy-dressed children with their red, wind-chapped legs showing above Wellington boots that I remembered from my youth, I saw ones dressed in mini teenage outfits, riding gleaming bicycles or cruising along on skateboards.

Hanging baskets decorated the freshly painted pubs, proclaiming that they were no longer only a male domain.

We arrived at our destination, a small seaside town that boasted not only window boxes and hanging baskets, but blackboards placed on pavements advertising 'pub grub'. Northern Ireland had moved into the twenty-first century.

We pulled up outside an old grey stone double-fronted Victorian house. Although its austere exterior had not been altered, it had been converted several decades earlier into a smart restaurant.

We entered and stepped back into another time. With its dark wood interior and heavy furniture, it had hardly changed since I had first visited nearly thirty years ago. Then I had been escorted by a boyfriend who had hoped to impress me as he had ushered me in. Unused to such splendour, I had searched the menu looking for a familiar dish to order, then sat in an agony of indecision as I wondered which cutlery to pick up first. Then I'd ordered chicken Kiev and a bottle of Mateus rosé wine, which I'd thought then was the pinnacle of sophistication. Now I was used to expensive restaurants and menus no longer frightened me.

I walked in with confidence and looked about. Regency-striped wallpaper, moss-green carpet and black-and-white clad waiters added to the old-fashioned ambience but those who knew the excellence of the innovative menu were not there in search of metal and glass interiors.

We went up to the receptionist and asked for a table.

'Certainly, ladies, this way please. I'll take you to the restaurant,' she said.

'Actually,' I said, 'could you show us into the bar?'

'Are you lunching with us?' the receptionist asked frostily. 'Would you not be more comfortable in the restaurant?'

Ladies at these establishments I knew ordered drinks, preferably a sweet sherry, at their table as they perused the menu. That wasn't for me.

'I want champagne and oysters first,' I declared. 'We'll have the meal later.'

The receptionist hesitated for a moment over this breach of etiquette but then showed us the way to the bar where we could sit at a small table in the window and enjoy our treat. 'Are you and your friend celebrating something?' she asked with a slight sniff of disapproval; she might not have been overloaded with charm but she still had her curiosity.

I could have told the truth and said, 'Yes, I'm celebrating my father's death.' But, not wanting to shock her, I took pity and said, 'We're just enjoying our holiday. And this place was very highly recommended to us. We're looking forward to sampling the menu – I've heard it's excellent.'

Her face softened. She obviously assumed that we were tourists from 'across the water' who knew no better, so she forgave our lack of decorum and showed us to a window seat.

For once my diet was to be forgotten, indulgence was the name of the game. The barman brought over the ice bucket holding the champagne and poured out two glasses. I raised my glass in a toast to my father.

'Thanks, Dad, for the first meal you've ever bought me!'

'To good old Joe,' murmured my friend and, grinning at each other, we clinked glasses conspiratorially. She knew the truth. It was why she had offered to come with me to Ireland and help me. An hour later the champagne bottle was empty, the oysters eaten and it was time to go to the restaurant. We had already ordered a Chateaubriand steak for two with all the accompaniments and a bottle of full-bodied red wine.

'Will one bottle be enough?' I asked my friend and saw with some amusement the look of consternation that crossed the waiter's face. Another thing that ladies do not do is get drunk in smart Irish restaurants. He was not to know that we were no strangers to wine and champagne. I was not bothered. I had already decided that we would get a taxi back and leave the car for later.

'Yes,' she replied firmly but relented when I ordered the cheese board. Afterwards we both agreed that Irish coffees were a must.

Three Irish coffees later, after we'd talked as old friends do when the hours seem like minutes, we suddenly noticed the day was fading and the restaurant was about to set up for the evening's customers.

'Time to pay the bill,' I said, and signalled for the waiter.

A look of relief crossed his face when he realized we were leaving and not ordering more drink. The bill was presented with discreet speed on a silver salver.

The receptionist reappeared complete with her original look of disapproval.

'Would that be your red car parked outside?' she asked.

I took the hint. 'Yes. Would it be all right if we left it here till the morning? We've enjoyed our meal so much we might have overdone it a little.' I could see that she heartily agreed. Still, my sensible caution, not to mention the generous tip, seemed to mollify her slightly and with a gracious nod she walked off to order a taxi.

She held the door open for us as we were leaving. Before we could go, a group of men entered. I knew them – they were members of my father's golf club.

'So sorry for your recent loss,' they murmured when they saw me. 'A terrible thing to lose your father.'

Behind me, I heard the shattering of illusions.

I went back to my father's house that evening. The funeral was the next day and the quicker the house was sorted out, the quicker I could leave town.

Only then would the past recede and free me from the thoughts of Antoinette that were flooding my mind. The pictures of her came one by one and unwillingly I felt my adult self being pulled back through the years.

Chapter Ten

Antoinette tried to ignore him, but she was aware that her father's eyes followed her every movement. Whatever she was doing – tidying her room, making the tea, watching television, going out to work – he was watching her.

When she was in the house, Joe expected his daughter to wait on him like an obedient little servant. Outwardly compliant, Antoinette was continually counting the hours until she could leave the house.

Meanwhile, her mother continued with the game of 'Daddy's been working away'. She acted as though he'd only been gone a week. The reality of what had led up to her husband's absence was a closed book. Ruth was determined that not only would there be no mention of the truth, but that the past was completely rewritten and her part in it whitewashed out. She had never stood by, wilfully blind and silent, as her husband abused their daughter over a period of years. It simply hadn't happened.

For Antoinette it seemed that the last two and a half years had vanished. Once again she had become a girl with very limited control over her life. Now that her parents were reunited as a couple, they had become powerful again while she was locked outside their magic circle, floundering on her own and completely at their mercy.

The lodge no longer felt like the home that Antoinette and her mother had created. Joe's presence had invaded it: overflowing ashtrays were left by the side of the wing armchair for his daughter to empty; newspapers, open on the sport pages, were tossed to one side while his cup stained with the residue of his numerous cups of tea, made for him by either Antoinette or her mother, sat on the coffee table. There was now a shaving mug in the kitchen and a grubby towel that Antoinette could not bear to touch lay on the draining board.

Just as two and a half years ago Ruth's happiness had been dictated by her husband's moods, so it was now. Her happy smile gradually faded, to be replaced by either frowns of discontent or the expression of the long-time sufferer that Ruth believed herself to be. Antoinette hardly ever heard her humming the tunes of her favourite songs now. Why couldn't her mother see it, she wondered. Had she forgotten the simple pleasures of the quiet, harmonious life that they had shared before *he* had come back? Why would she wish to be back in his control, the whole house governed by his moods and the aura of grim power that surrounded him? It seemed impossible to Antoinette that anyone would want to choose this existence over the one that they had enjoyed together before her father's release.

It wasn't as though there had been any material gain, either. Although her husband got a job as a civilian mechanic working for the army, and was given hours of overtime, somehow his contribution to the housekeeping did not appear to make Ruth's finances easier. In fact, with one more mouth to feed and the forty-cigarettes-a-day habit that Joe had, money seemed even scarcer.

Four weeks after he returned home, he announced that he had to work at the weekend. 'Leave early and back late,' he had said with his jovial smile.

'Oh Paddy,' she had protested, using her nickname for him, 'not on a Saturday. You know I've the weekend free.'

The coffee shop where Ruth was the manageress catered to the professionals who worked a five-day week and without their custom the owner had decided to close after lunchtime on Saturdays, a decision popular with both Ruth and her daughter.

Seeing the suspicious look that his wife was giving him, Joe's good-humoured expression changed to one of irritation.

'Well, we need the money, don't we? Sure, and aren't you the one who's always saying you want to move into a larger house in Belfast?'

Antoinette saw her mother's face take on the resigned expression that had become familiar over the last few weeks as she replied, 'Yes, dear.'

'Well, then, what're you complaining for? It's time and a half at the weekend. Maybe if that big daughter of yours contributed more instead of spending it all on those clothes and that damn stuff she puts on her face, I wouldn't need to work so hard.'

Antoinette waited for her mother to contradict his accusation. She had contributed to the running of the house ever since she had been able to. But Ruth said nothing.

Although she knew that Ruth had always yearned for a house similar to the one she had grown up in, a gracious Georgian three-storey building, it was the first time Antoinette had heard that plan voiced. It seemed to her that her father wanted to control everything, even where they lived.

The gate house was comfortable enough for us before he turned up, she thought resentfully. Working overtime is just another excuse to keep his wife quiet.

She mistrusted his story and, as she saw the triumphant look on his face as he won the short argument, she believed it even less. Knowing that her mother only pretended to accept his reasoning fuelled her resentment even more.

'Going to the greyhound races more like it,' she muttered under her breath.

Seeing the expression which had crossed his daughter's face and reading it correctly, Joe glared at her as he snapped, 'What are you doing standing there? Help your mother while I'm out – make yourself useful for once.'

With that parting shot, he left. The noise of the door slamming behind him vibrated in the now-silent room.

Ruth and her daughter glanced at each other and Antoinette could see the unhappiness on her mother's face. She hardened her heart to it, for she felt past trying to cheer her mother up. Just for once Ruth could have stood up for her daughter and pointed out that she contributed more than her fair share. She felt the injustice of his remarks and hurt by the usual lack of support from her mother. If she wouldn't stand up for her, who would?

Antoinette went to her room hoping that her father would win enough from the dog races to keep him away from the house until she had left for the evening. She knew that she had contributed as much to the housekeeping as he had. With her tips, she earned as much as he did – a fact that fuelled his simmering anger towards her.

She thought of how he commandeered the television she had bought and sat watching the sports programmes that she detested; how her mother cooked his favourite food, never asking Antoinette what she wished for; how, when her daughter had offered to cook an evening meal, he had jeered at her efforts calling it 'that dammed fancy muck of yours'. Since his return, except for that one unsuccessful attempt, she was reduced to doing the more menial task of washing up.

Antoinette had no wish to meet her father when she was dressed for her night out. She knew he would mock her attempts to look nice and knock her fragile self-confidence even further. If he was in a bad mood, she would be his target, a mental punch bag for him to unleash his anger on, anger that now always seemed to simmer close to the surface. Nor did she want to see the sadness on Ruth's face, though she could not help feeling that her mother had brought her misery upon herself. Antoinette could see no point in having someone in the house who created such a feeling of discord, and she could not understand why her mother had allowed him to return to his old ways in such a short space of time. She heard Joe's evasions, saw his smugness and watched her mother pandering to his wishes. She felt an increasing contempt for her parents as she saw his dominance and Ruth's acquiescence.

When her father was out, her mother would seek her out, keen for company and an ear she could complain into, but this time Antoinette was determined she would not relent and give in to her. Instead she spent the afternoon in her room deciding on which outfit she was going to wear for her night out and finally made her selection. She neatly laid out on the bed a pale yellow dress with a low-cut neck and a straight skirt that had a small back pleat which enabled her to walk freely while emphasizing her slim legs. The broad belt that she had chosen was covered with a darker fabric, which would encircle her waist tightly and make it look slimmer.

It's ever so sophisticated, she thought, satisfied with her choice.

She had bought it in one of the new boutiques that were opening everywhere, full of fashion for teenagers. This place was one of a chain brought over from England that had recently opened in the centre of Belfast. Middle-aged shop assistants had now been replaced with tall, slim model types who wore the fashions so beautifully that all the girls, whatever their size and shape, wanted to copy them.

She knew the other girls in her group would also have treated themselves to new outfits, for tonight was going to be a special event. There was a new band with a lead clarinet player called Acker Bilk appearing for the first time in Belfast. All the girls had talked excitedly about them. The band's first record had hit the charts and that alone had put them into a different league than the usual groups who had regularly performed in Northern Ireland.

Antoinette had arranged to meet her friends at seven thirty in their usual haunt, the coffee shop where only a few weeks ago she had met her father, though she tried not to think about that. It was an occasion that made her grimace with distaste every time she remembered it.

She was contentedly listening to the latest record by Elvis Presley, a new one she had bought. With a glass of vodka in one hand and a forbidden cigarette in the other, she squinted against the plume of smoke, she moved in time to the music. In her imagination she was already on the dance floor, receiving admiring looks as she put into practice the new steps she had learnt.

Judy, knowing that Antoinette's preparations were a prelude to leaving, eyed her dolefully from the nest she had made on the bed.

Antoinette checked the mirror again to see if her carefully applied make-up needed any finishing touches.

'Just some lipstick,' she said to herself, and then decided to wait until her drink was finished and the last drag of the cigarette taken. She wanted to savour these few moments. She felt relaxed and almost happy, for it seemed her wish had been granted and her father was not going to return until after her departure.

The volume of the music drowned out the sound of the front door slamming. Her short-lived peace was abruptly shattered by an angry roar and she knew at once, with a feeling of dread, that her father's afternoon drinking must have followed losses at the race track. He would only have come back early if he'd run out of money and the anger in Joe's voice as it carried up the stairs and invaded her room proclaimed that the day had not gone his way. Somehow that would be someone else's fault. It always was. Antoinette would, she knew, become the target of his unpredictable temper. Unable to ignore the fierce shout, she opened her bedroom door with trepidation.

'Antoinette, get yourself down here and turn that blasted music off, do you hear me?'

Reluctantly she shot back into her room, removed the record from the turntable and went downstairs. Her father stood at the bottom step, his face puce with alcohol-induced rage. Behind him she saw her mother, her face wearing its usual impassive expression, her mouth fixed in a small tight smile, as she sat in her chair watching her daughter and her husband.

Antoinette understood that as usual, there would be no help from that quarter and stood silently waiting to hear what her father wanted. Marring her pleasure in going out with her friends would be top of his list, for if he had not enjoyed his day, the thought of her enjoying her evening would be insufferable.

'Where do you think you're going with all that muck on your face, my girl?'

'Just to the local dance with my friends.' She hid her agitation and replied in a calm voice, hoping to placate his ill temper.

'Well, you look a sight. You're not leaving my house looking like that.'

He reached his arm out and pulled her roughly towards him. Gripping her chin and lifting her face, he studied it contemptuously.

Antoinette recoiled at the smell of his breath, and he felt her flinch but knew she was too scared to protest. Joe sneered while his fingers dug in to the sensitive flesh of her cheeks even harder. 'Go to the sink and wipe some of that damn make-up off,' he instructed.

She walked into the kitchen and did as she had been told, blinking away treacherous tears that threatened to slide down her cheeks. She quickly wiped some of her pan stick off, feeling his eyes following her. She looked at her face in the small mirror above the sink and watched the pretty girl she so longed to be disappear with each stroke of the damp flannel. She patted her face dry slowly, wanting to put off turning around to face her father; she knew that he had not finished tormenting her.

'Is that better?' she asked, as she swallowed her pride.

All she wanted to do was to appease him sufficiently to be able to leave the house without a full-scale row erupting. She knew that nothing would give him more pleasure than to find an excuse to ban her from leaving and send her to her bedroom.

'You still look a mess. You're getting fat as well.'

That dreaded word, feared by every fashion-conscious teenager, flew like a dart and landed with deadly accuracy in the centre of her confidence. She winced and Joe knew his barb had deflated her self-esteem. He gave her a contemptuous look and snorted.

'Don't you be coming home late, my girl. I want you back by eleven and not a minute later, do you understand?'

All signs of the self-assured teenager that had been reflected in her bedroom mirror only a few minutes ago had disappeared, leaving in her place an awkward nervous girl. Antoinette wanted to open her mouth and protest but she knew what the result would be if she did. She lowered her head instead and studied the carpet, not wanting to meet his eyes. She felt the heaviness of the silent pressure from both of her parents to answer.

'Yes, Daddy,' she replied in what she hoped were conciliatory tones.

Antoinette knew better than to argue that the dance did not finish until eleven or to protest that she would then have to queue for her coat and walk to the bus stop. She would just have to leave early and come home alone. The last part of the evening was to be denied her; the companionship of the other girls as they caught the last bus, laughing, chattering and reminiscing over the night's events.

Her father turned away, a complacent smile on his face. Now that he had won, it seemed that he was bored with taunting her.

She knew his rules were not made because he cared what time she came home, but because he demanded her total submission. And, just as when she was a child, her mother never interfered. She simply ignored it.

Antoinette saw the look of pleasure on her father's face as he felt her enjoyment of the night ahead diminish, then the smile faded and his malevolence showed through. He would have preferred a show of defiance from her so that he could have had the greater pleasure of banning her from going out.

On one occasion she had rebelled against his authority and had argued her point when he accused her of not helping in the home more. For that burst of insolence, as he had perceived it, she had been banished upstairs and forbidden to leave her room. That night Antoinette went to bed hungry while the smells of their supper cooking drifted up to her along with the sound of the television she had paid for.

She climbed back up the stairs and felt a wave of anger that turned into a surge of hatred that this time was directed at both her parents: her father for his arrogant bullying and her mother for her compliance. The anger added to her defiance and she hastily crammed all of her make-up into her handbag. She would fix her face on the bus, she told herself.

Taking consolation from that thought, she wriggled into her tan stockings and slipped on her yellow dress, clinching her belt tightly around her waist. Then she put on her pointed-toe stilettos and she was ready. Not wanting to give him the satisfaction of finding something else to sneer at, she hastily covered her outfit with a coat.

Determined that she would not be a target again of her father's derision and taunts or, worse, somehow annoy him further, she scurried from the house. She knew she would arrive in town early and have to sit on her own until her friends arrived.

'God, I hate him. Why can't he leave me alone?' she asked herself miserably as she walked to the bus stop, feeling her eyes well up with tears again. Angrily she brushed them aside.

She did not want what was left of her mascara to run down her cheeks and stain them with dark rivulets.

'Don't let him get you down,' she told herself. 'Enjoy tonight, you mustn't let him win.' Her shoulders straightened, her head was held higher and her step more purposeful as she heeded her own advice.

Chapter Eleven

Antoinette fixed a smile firmly on to her face as she entered the coffee bar. She did not want her friends to suspect there was anything wrong, or to know that for the last hour she had sat alone in a bar, ignoring the stares given to a single girl in a male-dominated environment as she ordered two double vodkas.

Cappuccino coffees were brought to the table as the girls talked about the new band, how good the clarinet player was and – even more exciting – how he had apparently learnt his skill in the army.

Their eyes widened at each piece of gossip and Antoinette laughed and giggled with the group, determined not to show that for her the excitement of the evening had been spoilt. Another round of coffees was drunk before the girls made their way to the Plaza, a smart dance hall in the centre of Belfast. It was a large building, brightly lit, with plush velvet seating and a bar lavishly decorated with mirrors. It was here that that live bands played the latest music for the city's youth to dance to on a Saturday night.

Tables and chairs ringed the large dance floor, a glitter ball spun its magic and with its smart seating and elegant décor, the Plaza had become the in place. Here the latest fashions and hairstyles were worn. The girls spent the afternoon before they went at the hairdressers, and the boys had discovered that Brylcream not only slicked hair back but with a little bit of work could turn neatly cut hair into fashionable quiffs made popular by their favourite pop stars.

Antoinette and her friends gave their coats to the cloakroom attendants then made a beeline for the ladies toilets. There they joined the mass of girls repairing make-up and admiring their reflections in the large mirrors. The final improvements to their appearances had to be inspected by their friends before they sauntered nonchalantly out to join in the melée outside.

The evening lived up to the group's expectations and they jived away to the up-beat tempo of the band alongside the hordes of youngsters who filled the dance hall. When the clarinet player lifted the instrument to his mouth and at the request of the audience released the haunting melody of 'Stranger on the Shore' for the second time, Antoinette danced slowly to the seductive notes of the hit tune. She hardly noticed her partner or heard what he was saying for one thought nagged at her: what excuse could she make for having to leave early?

At ten o'clock, she turned to one of her friends and said she had to go.

'What, already?' asked her friend, surprised. 'You'll miss the end of the dance. It's the best bit. Why do you have to leave so early? You don't usually have to go home before the rest of us.'

Antoinette's excuse came easily. She had spent the whole evening planning it, after all. 'I know, it's a shame, but my parents are taking me to Coleraine tomorrow. We're visiting my grandparents for lunch and then going on to my aunt, uncle and cousins, so we have to be up early for the drive. It'll take three hours, you know. So I've got to get bed at a sensible time tonight.' It was strange that she could lie so easily about her relationship with the family who had rejected her three years before.

Her friend nodded and shrugged. She didn't much mind whether Antoinette stayed or left. 'See you next week then. Bye,' was all she said before turning her attention back to the band.

Antoinette slipped away from the dance floor unnoticed and collected her coat from the cloakroom. At the bus stop she placed a wad of chewing gum in her mouth. Although she had swapped from whiskey to vodka some time ago, she felt safer with the smell of mint on her breath. Her mother might know that she drank but she would not let her father see any more weaknesses than he already did. Antoinette did not see any irony in that thought, for it was her father who had introduced her to whiskey when she was still a child.

As her father had instructed, she caught the early bus home which brought her back to the gate lodge well before the curfew that Joe had set. She wanted to deprive him of an excuse to complain about her behaviour.

He'll just have to find another excuse to bully me, she thought grimly.

Letting herself in quietly, she was relieved to find that both her parents appeared to be asleep, for the house remained silent as she crept up the stairs. She knew that if she had arrived later than the time demanded of her, Joe would somehow have known. Antoinette picked up Judy and placed her on the bed. When she'd got ready for bed, she climbed in next to her dog and cuddled her as she waited to fall asleep.

I hate him, she thought as she began to grow drowsy. She longed for life to go back to how it had been before he came home, but that, she knew, was impossible.

Antoinette patted the bed as an invitation for Judy to join her. Even though the little dog now suffered with rheumatism, the offer of joining her mistress on the bed was normally taken up with delight. This time, when she tried to clamber up, she slipped, falling back with a yelp.

Antoinette stretched her arms out and picked up the now elderly dog and settled her by her side. Judy gave another whimper and, suddenly worried, Antoinette looked for the source of her discomfort. She ran her fingers gently over her stomach which felt distended. Then near the bottom of it, she found a swelling that was small but hard.

'I'll take you to Mr McAlistair,' she said, more to reassure herself than her pet. 'He'll make you better.'

She gently stroked Judy as she whispered reassuring words into her ear and with a pang realized that the little dog's back-bone had become prominent, forming a fleshless ridge which her thick fur had until now hidden. Judy, she now realized fully for the first time, had become an old dog.

Antoinette cradled the confidante of all those childhood secrets whispered since her fifth birthday, and she kissed the top of the wiry head, flooded with love for her pet. Dogs, she knew, seldom live beyond twelve and Judy had nearly reached that birthday; but that knowledge did not make the reality any more bearable.

She felt a lump in her throat. Over the last six months since her father had come home, Judy had not just been the main reason she had continued to stay at home but the only good thing in it.

Even if she had been able to find a landlady prepared to rent to a teenager with a pet, she could not have taken an old dog away from her familiar surroundings and the small garden she was used to. What could she have offered in return? Only a life in a pokey bed sitter which was all she could have afforded. As cruel as her father was to her, he never took his spite out on the animals. No, he would stroke both Judy and the marmalade cat her mother adored, while he shouted at her.

Judy had been the one constant in Antoinette's life. Unlike the humans that had been part of her world, the dog had never faltered in showing unconditional love for her mistress. She had sat quietly by Antoinette when she had despaired of life, licked her hand with her dog kisses to show support, and in return Antoinette had loved her.

She looked into Judy's liquid brown eyes that returned her gaze with such trust and knew she had to do what was best for her pet. She gave her one more hug then went downstairs to telephone the vet.

Less than an hour later Antoinette heard the words she had been dreading ever since she found the lump.

'I'm sorry, Antoinette, the tumour is malignant.'

'Can you operate on her?' she asked, wanting to place her hands over Judy's ears to protect her from hearing her fate. From the vet's expression, she knew what the words were going to be. Instead she gently stroked Judy's head and braced herself for what was to come.

'She's an old dog – it wouldn't be fair on her to put her through it. You know even if we removed the growth it would come back again.'

'What can you do?'

'She's in pain, Antoinette, and it will get worse. You have to be brave and face up to it. I know how much you love her,' he continued gently, 'but it's the last thing you can do for her. You don't want her to suffer, do you?'

Antoinette pushed down the sobs that were threatening to leave her throat; she did not want Judy to feel her grief. The little dog, who always knew when her mistress was upset, looked up at her curiously.

'It's all right, Judy, your stomach won't hurt for long,' she whispered and then faced the vet again. 'When do you want to do it?'

'Tomorrow. I want you to have a nice evening with her, then first thing in the morning you give her a pill that will make her drowsy. Then you bring her into me at ten a.m. I'll give her an injection, and you can hold her until she goes to sleep. It's only after that that we bring her into this room for the final injection but by then she won't know anything. Her last memory will be of you holding her.'

'She won't feel anything, you promise?'

'No, Antoinette, she won't feel anything.'

Antoinette left the vet with Judy trotting by her side, trying not to think about life without the little dog's companionship.

When she got home, she explained to her mother, with a shaking voice and tears raining down her face, what the vet had said. For once, Ruth was supportive, and tried to comfort her even though Antoinette was inconsolable. Seeing her daughter's tears, Ruth's eyes filled as well, for she loved the little dog too.

Then, to Antoinette's amazement, her father said something entirely unexpected.

'Antoinette, I know how much you love your dog. Do you want me to take her for you in the morning? It's not easy you know, doing what you're doing.' Joe bent to stroke Judy, this time gently.

Antoinette looked at him for a moment with astonishment; then, when she realized he was sincere, with gratitude. 'Thank you, Daddy, but I want to do it for her. I want to be with her.'

Her father stood up and gently patted his daughter on the head. 'I'll tell you what, I'll go down the road, get us all some nice fish and chips, and your mother can make some tea. You sit with your wee dog.' With a smile that reminded her of the father she had once known when she was very young, Joe left.

He returned from the chip shop laden not just with large portions of fish and chips but with pickled onions and mushy peas as well. Ruth laid the table, cut thin slices of bread and butter, and they tucked into the feast. After the fish and chips, there were thick wedges of fruit cake, and while they ate they diluted the sadness of the day by sharing their memories of the little dog's life.

'Hey, do you remember the time Judy jumped from an upstairs window, when she was just a puppy?' asked Joe. 'I had to race to the vet with her and after all that, she hadn't even broken a bone. Just pulled a muscle. Still landed me with a large bill, though.'

They laughed, remembering how Judy had had her two front legs taped together while the muscle healed, and what a comical sight she had looked. Her strange appearance when taken for a walk did not in any way dent her enjoyment, nor did it stop her from jumping up with muddy paws on the furniture.

'And what about the time you hired her out to the local farmer to catch rats?' said Ruth. 'I was furious with you!'

But as they remembered the plucky little terrier's spirit, anger was forgotten and they laughed instead.

'She's had a good life, Antoinette,' her father said eventually. 'I'll clear the dishes away. You and your mummy go and watch a bit of television and I'll make us all a nice cup of tea.'

And for that evening, Antoinette was lulled into thinking that the game of happy families that Ruth had orchestrated over the years was a reality. It was those brief moments of happiness that encouraged her to perpetuate the myth that she was part of one.

That last night, Judy shared Antoinette's bed; she curled into the crook of her mistress's arm and hardly moved. When Antoinette opened her eyes early the next morning, Judy gave her a few gentle licks before snuggling back down contentedly on the bed. Antoinette picked her up and took her downstairs to let her out into the garden. There Judy squatted, savouring her morning ablutions, then leisurely sniffed a few clumps of grass before strolling back into the house.

Antoinette poured some of her tea into a saucer for her. Judy much preferred it to water and she lapped it up gratefully. When every drop had been licked from the bowl, she looked up at her mistress expectantly. Her tail wagged furiously when, to her delight, she was given another treat – a chunky piece of ham. It was there, wedged in the centre, that Antoinette had artfully hidden the pill. When Judy had eaten it, Antoinette picked her up and put her on her knee, running her fingers through Judy's coarse fur until she touched the lump that distorted the dog's stomach and traced gentle circles around it. She laid her smooth head against the rough fur of her pet, letting it tickle her face. Then she took the face of her childhood companion in both her hands, turned it towards her and saw the devoted expression there. She had received unquestioning love from Judy, who had managed to melt the cold frightened place in her heart and given her comfort when there was nothing from anyone else. So many times she cried into Judy's coat until the little animal had licked away her tears with doggy kisses.

Antoinette felt a pain in her chest that seemed to be a lump made of all the tears she had cried over the years. Where do they come from, she wondered. Is there a sac made of a thin membrane that our grief enters and becomes water, then, once filled, it finally bursts, releasing an unstoppable torrent?

When Judy's body grew heavy and her breathing deeper, Antoinette knew she had fallen into a light doze and it was now time to take her to the vet. She picked her up carefully, not wanting to waken her, and carried her on that short walk.

The vet opened the door, gave her a kind smile, and brought them quickly into the surgery.

'Antoinette, I'm just going to give her the first injection. Then she will simply slide into a deeper sleep. She won't feel anything.'

Fighting to control her emotions, she watched as the needle slid into the back of her dog's neck, then carried her gently back into the waiting room. There she sat, holding her pet and not letting herself think of the evening ahead when she would return to her parents alone. It seemed like only minutes but was in fact nearly an hour when the vet called her back for the final injection. He took the sleeping dog from Antoinette's arms and laid her on the table. She watched as the needle was placed in the dog's ankle. Still holding back her tears, she stroked the fur of Judy's head until she felt her grow limp and, as life left the little dog, she said a silent good-bye.

The tears streamed down her face as she walked the short distance to the gate lodge. She let herself into the house that now felt unbearably quiet and went straight to her bedroom.

Once there, she clutched her pillow for comfort and wept for the loss of the companion of her childhood.

Her only comfort was that she knew that she had returned the dog's love with this final gift, of allowing her to slide, secure in the love of her mistress, into a painless last sleep.

Chapter Twelve

Antoinette was going on her very first date and suddenly she felt like a carefree teenager. Derek wanted to take her for a meal in a new restaurant that had opened in Belfast. It was a Chinese one, the first there had been in the city, and Antoinette, who had only heard about this strange food, was excited at the thought of it.

At the dance hall in Belfast the Saturday before, a stocky blond man of about twenty had asked her for the first dance then hardly left her side. It was not until a slow tune was being played that he said, 'You don't remember me, do you? I danced with you nearly a year ago at the marquee in Lisburn.'

She looked more closely at him. 'Oh, yes! I remember you,' she said as she realized he was the round-faced boy who had led her on to the dance floor for the last waltz. 'You were a bit forward, weren't you?' she said, but smiled to show she didn't mean it nastily.

Derek smiled back at her and as the evening progressed, Antoinette realized that a year had changed him from a nice boy to a young man with social skills. He bought her soft drinks, none of which had a trace of the smuggled vodka that Antoinette had come to like but she was having too good a time basking in the admiration she could see in his face to care. Her eyes sparkled back at him. She liked the way he looked. In his sports jacket and cord trousers, he was different from the crowd she was used to.

'I've been looking out for you ever since that night we danced together,' he confided to her.

'Really?' It was hard to believe. She was more used to trying to avoid sweaty hands when their owners had become worse for drink than having an admirer seek her out with real interest. She felt dazzled by him – he was no boy looking for a quick grope, but a young man who wanted to get to know her properly and spend time with her. When he asked her if she would be interested in going out for dinner with him, she was overwhelmed and tried to hide her excitement as she accepted.

It was the first time she had been asked out for a proper date, something she knew all the girls who made up her group at the dances hoped for. She wanted to share her pleasure with her mother, wanted her to be happy for her but some instinct told her that Ruth would not be pleased.

The weeks since her husband's return had taken their toll and now Ruth's face seemed permanently set into an expression of discontent. The good humour that her husband had shown on the eve of Judy's death had quickly faded and once again he was seldom home at the weekends without giving any reasons.

If Derek had only wanted to take me out on a Saturday, she thought, as she went home that night. Then I wouldn't have to tell my mother or my father anything about it. But there's no excuse I can come up with for being out late on a week night. No – I'll just have to tell her, and hope that she gives me permission.

She knew that the reason she was allowed out on a Saturday night was not just because that concession had been granted before her father had returned. Although he might have liked to stop her he had not yet come up with a good enough excuse as he knew very well that Antoinette's contribution to the household bills eased the burden on him. If he pushed her too far and she left, he might have to increase his own contribution.

As she had so many times, Antoinette wished she had a normal family. She longed to have two parents who wanted what was best for her, instead of a father who tormented her with his bullying and a mother who had little interest in anything except keeping the peace at the cost of her daughter's happiness.

I could make something up to explain why I want to go out, Antoinette thought. I could tell her I'm going to the cinema with a girlfriend ... No, it's no good. She knows I don't have any close girlfriends. She'd never believe me. She'd make me say who it is, ask me to bring her to the coffee shop to meet her ...

The girls in Antoinette's group only met to frequent the dances, as it was impossible to go to dance halls alone, and they had little contact with each other outside their socializing, as Ruth knew very well. It would be hard to fake a sudden friendship.

At sixteen, Antoinette knew friendship was dangerous. It brought with it questions and she didn't want to give answers about her past or her present. She seldom allowed herself to feel any loneliness or to want the friendship of another girl of a similar age. She remembered only too well how the girls at her school, some who had known her for several years, had turned against her when the facts of her pregnancy came to light.

Antoinette understood that the girls she went to the dances with would disappear from her life the moment they had a boyfriend. She accepted their lack of interest in her and felt relief that she aroused so little curiosity.

I'll tell her, she decided, and then see what happens.

The next day, she found her mother on her own in the kitchen.

'I've been asked out,' Antoinette said, as casually as she could. 'A young man named Derek wants to take me to dinner on Thursday. I said I could go. Is that all right?'

Watching carefully, she saw conflicting emotions on her mother's face: there was worry and fear, as well as a reluctance to refuse Antoinette such a simple and normal request.

What is my mother so afraid of, she wondered. She knew that they were both afraid of her father, in their different ways, but nevertheless she had the instinctive feeling that there was another aspect to her mother's fears. After all, normal friend-ships and normal relationships meant questions that Antoinette would have to answer. Perhaps, one day, Antoinette would tell someone the truth and the whole carefully constructed edifice, the life that Ruth had tried so hard to build and to believe in, would come crashing down.

Antoinette watched her struggle with her doubts, but then Ruth relented with a sigh. 'All right, you can go. I can see how much you want to, and as you've already said yes, I don't suppose I can stop you.' Then she added, 'But I think it would be better if Daddy thought you were just going to the cinema with a girlfriend. Get this boy to bring you back to the coffee shop after the meal as I'm working the evening shift so you can come home with me.'

'All right then. Thank you, Mummy.' If that was the price of a night with Derek, then she was willing to pay it, even though she had been looking forward to being driven home to the gate lodge in Derek's car. Deep down, she knew her mother wanted to keep the peace within the house and that once again Ruth had taken the easy option of becoming an accomplice to her husband by pandering to his dominance.

She pushed aside the niggling question of why her father would have minded her having a date to the back of her mind. She also avoided asking herself why her mother had suggested hiding the fact from him. Deep down she knew the answers to both and she was not ready to cope with those answers yet, so she pushed them away and hid them from herself.

The night before her dinner date, Antoinette inspected her wardrobe, looking for a suitable outfit and discarding dresses one by one. She looked finally at her favourite yellow dress but Derek had already seen her in it, so that was no good. Like most girls of her age who loved clothes, she valued quantity over quality: shopping and being seen in new outfits was what mattered. Feeling that the clothes she had worn to the weekly dances would not be quite suitable, she persuaded herself without much difficulty to break into her savings. She had already found there is nothing quite as seductive as new clothes wrapped in tissue then placed in a smart carrier bag with the logo of a well-known boutique emblazoned on the side.

The next day she left the house early to go to the boutique where she had already seen the outfit she wanted on an elegant mannequin in the window. On the way, she kept her fingers crossed that the two-piece she had her eye on would still be there and, more importantly, that it would be in her size. She arrived at the shop one minute after opening time and saw to her relief that the coveted outfit was still there. Once the shop assistant had taken it off the mannequin, she found to her delight that it was a size twelve, her size.

As she preened in front of the mirror in it, she felt it was just the perfect outfit for her date: a straight navy skirt with a matching jumper trimmed with white cuffs and a large white sailor collar.

My white shoes and matching handbag will be perfect with it, she thought as she handed over the money. Then she went to Woolworth's and browsed through their Rimmel range. She chose a pale pink lipstick of a similar colour to the half a dozen she already owned. Finally she treated herself to a bottle of Blue Grass perfume and, delighted with her purchases, took herself for a coffee at a nearby café.

There she sat, surrounded by her bags, lost in a dream that she had been welcomed into smart society. She was invited to parties where, dressed in fabulous clothes, she was the centre of attention. She saw herself glass in hand, elegant in high heels, regaling a crowd of admirers with witty stories. Other girls, with envious eyes, asked her for fashion tips.

She came back to earth when she glanced at her watch and saw it was time to go to the coffee shop to commence her lunchtime shift. At work, tables had to be laid, cutlery polished and glasses wiped but all the time Antoinette had a wide smile plastered to her face as she served and cleared tables. She couldn't stop thinking about the evening ahead.

Derek was going to collect her from the coffee shop. Work finished at five thirty; she had made an appointment at the hairdressers next door, for she wanted her hair as well as her clothes to be perfect. Her make-up could be done in their mirror while her hair was being blow-dried and tweaked into shape. Then she could change at the coffee shop and sit with a frothy coffee in front of her, looking nonchalant while she waited for Derek to arrive.

Her mother had arrived for the evening shift when Antoinette returned with her hair freshly styled and her make-up carefully applied.

'How do I look, Mummy? Do you like my new outfit? Do you think Derek will like it?' she asked.

'Very nice, darling,' was Ruth's only comment, and she had to be content with that.

Derek turned up at exactly on time and Antoinette introduced him to Ruth. Ruth was the manageress and, unlike the waitresses who had to wear uniforms, wore her own clothes. Derek smiled as he was introduced to her, clearly at ease with her.

She must look like his mother's friends, thought Antoinette with relief, seeing acceptance on his face. She felt proud of her mother that evening: Ruth's refined accent and smart suit gave the impression that her background was not just respectable and middle class, but safe. After all, normal parents would care about their teenage daughter and want to protect her; they would want to meet the man who was taking their daughter out and expect their curfew to be kept.

Ruth seemed to know what Antoinette wanted from her, and instinctively became the gracious lady handing the care of her daughter over to someone else for the evening. It was a mother Antoinette was seeing for the first time. As she left she felt like any other teenager on her first date.

The restaurant was everything that she had heard it was. Other restaurants in Belfast favoured brick walls adorned with hunting prints but this place was painted magnolia, and the pictures were of white-faced women with startling red lips, wearing elaborate clothes. Their abundant black hair pinned into large knots exposed long delicate necks while their slender hands clasped richly coloured fans. The pictures of the exotic women from another continent and the strange tinkling background music captivated her as she felt she had been given a glimpse of a different culture; one far older and more mysterious than her own.

'This is lovely,' said Antoinette, as they were shown to their table.

'I'm glad you like it,' said Derek. 'Would you like a drink?'

He ordered some wine and then the menus came. When the menu was placed in front of her, Antoinette was bewildered by the list of meals that bore very little similarity to anything she had ever eaten before. Seeing her confusion, Derek gallantly offered to order for her and within a few minutes small china bowls filled with a clear chicken soup thickened by sweetcorn arrived.

She put the large china spoon into her mouth and gingerly swallowed. A smile of pleasure lit her face. It's delicious, she thought, simultaneously surprised and delighted: if it's all like this, then I think I must like Chinese food.

After the soup came something called chop suey. To cater for taste buds of Northern Ireland, a fried egg had been placed carefully on top. She poured a small amount of soy sauce on the side of her plate, scooped up the food with some difficulty and, as she placed it in her mouth, beamed with pleasure.

'You enjoying yourself?' Derek asked with an equally broad smile.

She nodded, and wondered what he would say if he knew that this was not only her first Chinese meal but the first time she had ever been on a date. But, with female wisdom, she withheld that piece of information. Maybe she would tell him when she got to know him a little better. Instead they talked, a little stiffly, about the dances they had been to and the kind of music they liked. They were little more than teenagers but they were trying to be adults, talking in the kind of way they thought adults did.

After she had swallowed her second sticky liqueur and drunk her final cup of coffee, it was time to go. After all, she had a curfew to keep and she knew, as Derek helped her on with her coat, that he respected her more for it. She felt her cheeks glow with pleasure when he suggested taking her out that Saturday. There was a film he suggested she would like and, not caring what it was, she readily agreed.

She returned to the coffee shop in time to meet her mother.

'Did you have a good evening, dear?' asked Ruth when she saw Antoinette.

'Oh yes, it was wonderful,' she replied happily. 'We had a terrific meal ...'

She was bursting to tell her mother all about her date, but her mother interrupted her. 'Good. But, you know, it's better if you don't tell your father what you've been up to. It would only cause trouble. Perhaps you'd better change out of those clothes before we go home. You understand, don't you, Antoinette? There's no need to make your daddy upset.'

The excitement began to die away as she looked at her mother. Ruth couldn't quite meet her gaze and Antoinette sensed that she was struggling to explain why her husband would not like his daughter having a date. Ruth was finding it difficult to pick her words and for once she did not give her the opportunity to voice them. Nothing was going to spoil her night.

Chapter Thirteen

Three months after their first date, Derek told Antoinette that he wanted her to meet his closest friends.

'Neil and Charlotte have been dating for a couple of years,' he explained. 'Charlotte lives at home, as you'd expect, but Neil is in his final year at Queen's and shares a flat with two other students near the university. I thought it would be nice if we went out as a foursome. What do you think?'

'That sounds lovely,' said Antoinette, though at once she felt panicky about whether Derek's friends would like her or not. She decided immediately that she would wear the same navy-blue two-piece suit that she had worn when Derek had taken her to the Chinese restaurant. Since then she had seen him regularly and so far had been able to hide from her father the fact that she had a boyfriend, although she was beginning to find the whole situation rather stressful. She'd see Derek on a Saturday night when they went dancing, and then sometimes on a Sunday when she sneaked out to meet him. They would go for a walk or to the cinema, and then have a kiss and cuddle afterwards. It was all very normal stuff, and so far she had managed to avoid him bringing her home, but she didn't know how much longer she'd be able to hide Derek's existence.

This time, on the night that they were going out with Neil and Charlotte, she agreed that he could fetch her from her home. As her mother was working the evening shift and her father was playing at a snooker match, she would have the house to herself. Joe would stay out until at least midnight, celebrating with his friends if he won or commiserating with them if he didn't. Whichever it was, she would not see him and he would be unaware of her plans for that evening.

As she got dressed, she realized how nervous she felt. After all, if Derek wanted her to meet his friends, it was a sign that their relationship was beginning to become serious. Knowing that, she still had fought against the temptation to buy another new outfit. I've got to save for secretarial college, she told herself sternly. It was still her dream to get the qualifications she needed to escape.

She washed her hair and styled it, carefully applied her make-up, then gave her suit a good brush down before squirting herself liberally with perfume. She was ready, but there was still half an hour before her boyfriend was due to arrive. She liked the word boyfriend and kept repeating it in her mind, feeling a warm glow spread inside her every time she did. She listened carefully for the sound of Derek arriving, and when she heard the car door slam, she rushed to open the front door.

Instead of the big old car he had driven before, Derek had drawn up outside her house in the smallest car she had ever seen.

'What sort of car is that?' she asked. She had never seen anything like it before.

'It's a Mini,' he replied. 'They've only just come on the market.'

'Isn't it lovely?' she exclaimed, walking round it and examining it. 'It's so little!'

'Do you like it?' asked Derek.

'Oh, yes,' she replied, hearing the pride and pleasure in Derek's voice at her surprise. 'I think it's beautiful.'

He opened the passenger door for her with a flourish. She perched herself on the seat and swung her legs into the car with a movement she had seen illustrated in a magazine article on how to climb in and out of a car gracefully. Once she was seated he jumped into the driving seat, slammed his foot down on the accelerator and the tiny car gave a full-size roar as they drove off.

I've finally arrived, she thought happily. This must be the most desirable car in Belfast. Her knees almost touched the dashboard, and her elbow nudged the window, but nothing took away the thrill of being seen in something so chic. This was a car for the fashionable young and she was in it!

They drove through Belfast to the popular Candle Light Inn, a large restaurant and bar on the outskirts of the city. Derek quickly parked and they both got out. He took her arm in a proprietary way and led her inside to the bar.

His friends were already there. As soon as she saw them, Antoinette felt uncomfortable.

Charlotte was dressed simply in a grey skirt and pale-yellow twin set with low-heeled leather pumps. Her hair fell in natural waves and, except for a touch of pink lipstick, her face was bare of make-up. Neil wore a sports jacket and twill trousers. In their smart casual clothes, Derek's friends had the aura of a carefree, comfortable and sophisticated life. Antoinette wanted to hide her white stilettos under the barstool. Suddenly her outfit felt cheap and her make-up too heavy.

As Derek made the introductions, she saw something else that made her heart sink. Knotted under Neil's collar was a tie she recognized. It belonged to the boys' grammar school in Coleraine – her father's home town.

Neil's older than me by several years, she thought, as fear crept over her. She did a quick bit of mental arithmetic. He would have been in his first year at university when the scandal about her broke out in Coleraine. Still, the sight of that tie made her nervous. No matter how much she tried to reassure herself, seeing that striped piece of fabric only inches from her face gave her a creeping dread that her secret was going to be exposed. She could still see the paragraph in the newspaper which informed the town of her father's crime and her disgrace. It began: 'Joseph Maguire, a mechanic residing in Coleraine, was today sentenced to four years for a serious offence against a minor.' Although, as she was under age, her name was excluded from the paper, the whole town had been aware of whom the minor was. They knew, passed judgement and closed their doors to her.

She grasped her drink tightly, then took a deep swallow to try and stop her anxiety. She had seen rejection on too many faces not to know the result when people discovered her past. Stop it, she told herself. Just concentrate on enjoying the evening.

'So what do you do?' Neil looked friendly and interested as he asked the question that she had been dreading.

'Oh, I'm taking a secretarial course next year,' she replied airily. 'At the moment I'm helping my mother run a coffee shop.'

Please don't ask me what my father does or where I went to school, she prayed and it seemed that her prayers were answered, for, after a few minutes of polite small talk, the men were more interested in talking about sport than delving into her past. She was left to have a stilted conversation with Charlotte, who was also thinking of taking a similar secretarial course once she had taken her final examinations at school.

'Why don't you take your course this year as well?' she asked.

'Because I've not saved up enough money' was the truthful answer but not one Antoinette wanted to give. She improvised hastily. 'Oh, it was that or hotel management so my mother suggested I took a year to think about it.'

Feeling she had handled that question without too many problems, she took another gulp of her drink, emptying her glass as she did so. Seeing her empty glass, Derek immediately ordered another round. He and Neil were drinking beer and Charlotte a Babycham. Without thinking, Antoinette asked for a vodka, her confidence-booster drink. Derek ordered it for her without question and she guzzled that one down quickly as well, then kept her hand over the glass in an attempt to hide its sudden emptiness.

A wave of depression engulfed her. These people had the life she had hoped for. It was only three years since she had been confident that she would go to university but that dream had shattered. Instead her education had been abruptly halted when she had been expelled from school. As soon as the authorities had learned what had happened to her, she was asked to leave immediately. If she had been able to stay on and study as she had planned, she would be one of them. As it was, the years since she had been forced to leave school had changed her from the studious girl who had taken pride in her school work to one who felt she had very little in common with those who were able to further their education.

The feeling of being out of place stayed with her all evening and later, in the restaurant, Antoinette hardly tasted the meal that was served. The room seemed to be stifling. The waiter kept topping up her glass as she drank the wine at a much faster pace than the others. She felt Derek glance at her as he noticed her consumption. She was embarrassed by it but still was unable to stop lifting the glass to her mouth.

After they'd all finished, Neil suggested that they have a final drink at the bar. Antoinette felt her head beginning to swim and as she walked the short distance to the bar her legs wobbled slightly in heels that now seemed even higher. She perched herself on the velvet bar stool, tucked her legs under it and tried to appear sober. Then, as she tried to follow the friendly buzz of conversation around her, the hairs on the back of her neck began to rise.

Suddenly she had the unnerving feeling that someone in the bar was watching her. She could feel eyes boring into her and reluctantly turned round.

It was her father.

He was standing with a group of men she had never seen before. Only a few feet separated her from him; the malevolence of his glare travelled across the distance between them. Completely unnerved, she turned back to her companions, gave a shaky smile and picked up her drink which she promptly downed in a single swallow.

'Would you like another one?' asked Neil courteously.

She sensed Derek's growing disapproval. This was her third large vodka of the evening but the need she felt for it was stronger than her desire to please him.

'Yes, please, same again,' she replied with some bravado.

'Charlotte?' asked Neil.

'Something soft for me, thanks,' she said, adding quickly, 'I've got studies to do tomorrow.'

Antoinette did not understand that the girl was trying to be kind to her with this excuse. Instead the word 'studies' just made her feel more wretched.

'Oh, I'm free until tomorrow afternoon,' she retorted in a voice she knew had become too loud. Then her neck prickled again. She felt her father's presence behind her even before she turned fully around to face him.

Joe stood in front of her. 'Antoinette, I want a word with you,' he said. Not acknowledging her companions, he scowled and beckoned her to follow.

She slid off her seat and obeyed, with a sense of foreboding.

Antoinette saw her father as her new friends would see him: a middle-aged man whose bloodshot eyes and flushed cheeks proclaimed him to be the drunk he was; an ignorant man, flashily dressed, who moved with the wide-legged walk of someone who thinks he appears sober; a drunk with a belligerent scowl and the harsh voice of the uneducated. She was instantly aware that he would never be welcomed in her friends' homes.

'What do you think you're doing with that nancy boy and his friends?' he asked. She saw his fist clench and knew he was restraining himself with difficulty from raising it to her. 'Get yourself home to your mother.'

Antoinette clenched her fists in an imitation of his but in her case it was to control her fear.

'Derek's taking me home soon,' she replied, knowing there was nothing she could say to appease him. She could see in his eyes the real reason for his rage. It was jealousy. The law might have punished him for his crime but the wish to commit it was still there. Lurking in his eyes was an expression that belonged to something foul that lived within him.

'Well, you go straight home, do you hear me?'

Derek appeared at her side. 'Are you all right?' he asked with concern in his voice. He had only met Antoinette's mother and her charming smile and refined voice had evidently given no hint that she was married to the kind of man standing in front of him now.

'Derek, this is my father, Joseph Maguire,' she said quickly, praying that her father's bad humour would not stop him being polite. 'Daddy, this is Derek.'

Joe ignored Derek's outstretched hand and glared at the young man, who involuntarily took a step back. Then it appeared that some thought of self-preservation entered Joe's head. At the same time, both he and Antoinette noticed two men in dark suits, the unobtrusive security staff, watching the tableau unfold before them. After a moment, he contented himself with giving a snort of derision and then said in a voice which shook with barely controlled temper, 'You bring her straight home now – and don't be buying her any more drink!'

With that, Joe turned abruptly on his heel and walked away with that slightly drunken walk, his neck brick red with im- potent rage. In his wake there was an appalled silence. Antoinette felt a flush creeping up her face – she knew every- one had heard what he had said – and she tried miserably to ease her humiliation with nervous chatter as she walked back to her seat.

She saw herself as she felt they all did: a girl dressed in cheap clothes wearing too much make-up; a girl who had drunk too much – as her father so obviously had as well.

They must see me as the daughter of a loud-mouthed, vulgar bully, she thought despairingly. And if his oil-stained, working man's hands didn't proclaim that he wasn't one of them, then his bad manners certainly did.

'Come on, Antoinette, I'll take you home.' Derek took her arm and held it firmly, more to make sure she walked in a straight line than to show affection, while she swayed and wobbled on her stilettos.

The car had hardly left the car park when she felt waves of nausea rising.

'Stop the car, I'm going to be sick!'

Her words had immediate effect – there was no way Derek was risking his new Mini. The car came to a swift halt and he reached over her to open the passenger door and push her head out over the pavement.

Antoinette vomited on to the street and then wiped her mouth with a tissue. Sinking back into her seat, she wondered if anything else could possibly go wrong. Then another wave of nausea gripped her and she jerked her head back over the side of the car to be sick again.

Tears ran down her face, taking streaks of mascara with them.

'Are you finished?' asked Derek.

'I think so,' she whispered, ashamed.

'Wind your window down,' he instructed tersely. 'The air might stop you being sick.'

She knew that Derek's concern was more for the interior of his new car than for her feelings. They set off again, speeding along the winding country roads back to Lisburn. Antoinette sat huddled up beside him, her arms folded across her chest for warmth, and the rest of the journey passed in silence. She felt completely wretched by the time the car drew up outside the gate lodge.

'Here we are then,' he said coldly, when they'd arrived. Then, seeing Antoinette's stricken face, he seemed to take pity on her. 'Look, it's a shame that the evening wasn't as successful as I'd hoped. I know you're upset by your father but his behaviour's not your fault.' He paused and then added, 'He did have a point about how much you'd drunk, you know.'

She took some consolation from the fact that Derek put her father's behaviour down to anger at her inebriated state, not to the fact that she was out with him.

'You really shouldn't drink so much,' he said. He leant over and opened the door for her. It was no surprise that he didn't kiss her – who would want to kiss someone who had just been sick? – but he made no mention of wanting to see her again either. Antoinette felt a sinking feeling in the pit of her stomach. Of course he wouldn't want to see her again after this – why would he? She could hardly blame him. And it had only been a matter of time before he discovered who she really was.

She climbed out of the Mini and walked unsteadily up the pathway that led to the house, hearing his car drive away before she opened the door. She looked round and saw his tail lights vanishing as his car turned a bend in the road and disappeared from sight. Antoinette felt miserably that with his departure he took the passport to the life she wanted.

Chapter Fourteen

For the next two days, Antoinette went around in a haze of dejection. On the third day Derek rang her. To her surprise, he was back to his usual kind and friendly self. His voice had none of the disapproval of a few days ago. Would she like to go out as usual this Saturday?

Her gloom disappeared and her spirits soared at the reprieve. She and Derek were still a couple – once again, she was a member of the privileged group of girls who had a boyfriend. She didn't have to worry about spending Saturday nights at dance halls with the remaining girls in the group. The few who had not yet been successful in finding a boyfriend seemed more desperate every week.

Thank goodness that's not me, she thought with relief. She had got used to going out with Derek. There wasn't much thrill to be had getting ready to meet her girlfriends any more. The very thought of going to the dance halls with them had become depressing instead of exciting; she wanted to spend her Saturday nights with her boyfriend. It was so wonderful to be with someone she could talk to, who valued her and looked at her appreciatively. When she saw that look of admiration in his eyes she felt special.

Antoinette felt the first stirrings of love. It was exciting and frightening at the same time, and with it came a compulsion to confide in him. She wanted what most people want – to be loved for herself. She wanted Derek to know her, understand her life, then take her away from it and throw a thick cloak of protectiveness over her. She loved the feeling of being protected that she had when he kissed her and cuddled her – it never went any further than that, and it never occurred to her that it would, nor did she want it to. She was happy with things as they were.

The fantasy of a wonderful life where Derek cherished and protected her kept her company as she counted the hours till she saw him again. It was the last thought she had before she went to sleep and the first one when she awoke. One day, she hoped, this dream would become reality.

Antoinette started getting ready for her date with Derek on Saturday afternoon. As she washed her hair at the kitchen sink, she felt a rising excitement at the thought of seeing him. The usual dreams of the two of them living together, of safety and protection far away from her father, floated through her mind. She was a little hazy on exactly what living with Derek would entail. Antoinette, with all her experience of one side of life, had very little knowledge of the other side. She didn't know much about adult relationships and her mother had never prepared her for growing up. Her knowledge had been gleaned from magazines and the fleeting company of the girls she had gone to the dances with and, at just under seventeen, she was far more naïve then her contemporaries. She could only imagine an indistinct fairy-tale scenario where she and Derek would live together happily ever after.

Now, with her date only a few hours away and her expectations running high, she had chosen her clothes and was enjoying painting her nails as she sprawled in front of the television.

Her mother was making tea and her bad humour could be read from the way she banged the crockery and her occasional snappish comment to her daughter.

'Make sure you are in early. Your father doesn't like you out late.'

Antoinette took no notice. Nothing was going to dent the pleasure of seeing Derek again. She watched *Juke Box Jury*, humming tunelessly along to the songs she recognized as she contently imagined her new life.

Her father had not mentioned the previous Saturday night again, and if anything he had seemed in a good humour the few times she had seen him since. Perhaps his fit of temper in front of her friends had defused some of his anger towards her. Whatever it was, Antoinette treasured the temporary lull in hostility.

She was startled when the door burst open and her father strode in heavily – the music had drowned out the sound of his car pulling up. She saw at once that his good humour had vanished. He smelt of drink and was scowling nastily at her.

'What do you think you're doing sitting around like that?' he asked as he took in the fact that she was only wearing her dressing gown. His mouth quivered with anger and she quickly scrambled to her feet, clutching the edges of her gown as she did so. 'And switch that damn television off – I don't want to watch a lot of idiots dancing round to jungle music.'

'Oh, come on, Daddy, it's the only thing I watch. You've always got the sports on when you're in. I did buy it, you know.'

He looked furiously at her as her words sunk in. It only took a moment for him to react; his face turned almost purple with rage at the thought she had dared answer him back. A dark flush crept from chin to forehead, even tingeing the whites of his eyes with colour. Spittle flew from his mouth as he shouted in a voice that shook with fury, 'Don't you be telling me what to do in my house, my girl!'

Seeing the unmistakable menace on his face, she tried to move but she had left it too late. Antoinette cringed with fear as she saw his hand clench. She knew that she had gone too far and that his rage was now unleashed. The thick fingers of one hand grasped her shoulder while the other one swung back and hit her in the chest.

Tears of pain and fear blinded her as she gasped for breath. It was the first time he had touched her since he had been released from prison. Before then he had been vicious and violent towards her but since his prison stint Antoinette had believed that fear of reprisal would stop him. It seemed not. She could hear his rapid breathing and smell his sweat, and she shook with terror.

His eyes slid down her body, fixed on the gap in her dressing gown and a sudden gloating expression came over his face, a look she recognized from her childhood. He knew she was naked underneath. It was an expression of lust but something even worse lurked in its depths: it was an overwhelming need to inflict pain.

When she was a child, he had believed that she was his possession to do what he wished with. That belief had resulted in a prison sentence. In those split seconds, as their eyes met, she prayed that he would remember that.

He did.

With a snort of what sounded like disgust, he thrust her away from him. She staggered back but a rage came from some part of her. She finally wanted to retaliate. For the first time she was not prepared to seek meekly the safety of her room. Sickened by his expression that made her feel soiled, she felt an answering fury burst out of her in a scream.

'You touch me and I'll tell the police! Go on! I dare you!'

At that moment, she wanted this confrontation, wanted him to hit her and the police to be called. Even the thought of being beaten did not deter her. No sooner had the words left her mouth, then his control snapped.

He pulled her towards him and as his fist rose in the air to inflict another blow, her mother stepped in between them.

Small as she was, Ruth was not frightened of the man she had married nor was she scared for her daughter. But she was scared of scandal and Antoinette was only too aware of what had motivated her mother to intervene.

'Don't, Paddy,' she said urgently as she laid a hand on his arm.

Her voice seemed to calm him and he stopped, panting, and lowered his fist. He let go of Antoinette, pushing her away from him, and glared at her. Then he said to his wife in a voice of fury, 'I want her out of the house, to be sure, when she starts that damn secretarial course she keeps talking about. She'll expect us to keep her, no doubt. Well, she can go to those friends of hers she thinks are so important. Where's she going tonight? You've let her have her way too long.' As the words left his saliva-flecked mouth, a tidal wave of rage overcame him. He no longer seemed to fear reprisals as he brushed Ruth to one side, grabbed his daughter again and shook her. 'I want you out of this house – you've caused enough trouble!' he roared. 'You're to pack and leave, do you hear me?'

And with that he dragged her to the stairs and shoved her up them. As she hurriedly clambered up, trying to escape, he aimed another blow at her back. She ran upstairs to the shelter of her bedroom and threw herself on the bed. From below, she could hear his voice still raised in anger, then her mother's softer tones as she tried to placate him. She heard the front door slam and the engine of his car start up, announcing his departure.

A few minutes passed, then there was the sound of her mother's steps on the stairs. The door opened and Ruth came into her bedroom.

Antoinette was sitting on the bed, her mind a blank. As usual, when her father began his aggression against her, she shut down all her emotions and responses. It was the only way to cope. Nevertheless, as her mother entered, she raised her eyes hopefully. Surely Ruth would see her husband for what he really was now. He had hit her, threatened to throw her out, for the smallest of reasons. Was that fair or just?

One look at her mother's cold face dashed any expectations she had. Any remaining hope that Ruth would take her side died completely with her mother's opening words.

'Antoinette, do you have to annoy your father so? I'm tired of trying to keep the peace. I've spoken to him and he's agreed that you can stay here until you go to Butlins. That's in two weeks. You'll save plenty of money there so you can get a bedsitter in town when you return. I can't have you both under the same roof. You just can't stop yourself upsetting him, can you? It's because you are so alike, I suppose.'

'Alike?' she echoed in disbelief.

'Yes, dear, you take after the Maguires. You always want to be out, you can't control your tempers and you're both selfish.' She saw the shocked look on her daughter's face at this character assassination and hastily continued. 'Oh, yes, dear, you are. Look at how many times when Daddy was away you left me sitting here alone. Still, we won't talk about that. He's my husband and you are quite old enough to fend for yourself so it's you that will have to leave.' She sat down on the edge of the bed and said more gently, 'It's better this way. You can come and visit, of course. It's just I want you to get your own place.'

And Antoinette understood that, once again, that her mother had made her choice.

After her mother had left, she stayed on the bed, staring sightlessly at the ceiling. She was transported back to her early years, when she was small, terrified and absolutely helpless. The frightened child was back, desperate for someone to take away the pain and fear and to make her feel better. Surely there was someone who could help her.

Yes, she thought. There is someone. I'm not alone anymore. I'll tell Derek, that's what I'll do. He cares for me. He wants to protect me. I know he'll help me and make me feel safe.

Comforted by the thought, she allowed a small smile to cross her face. At last, there was someone who could take away her burden.

Chapter Fifteen

Derek put his arms around her as she wept. She had thrown herself into the front seat of the Mini and the minute she was in the safety of the car, she had given way to her misery with shoulder-shaking sobs.

'What's wrong, Antoinette? What is it?' he said with a worried expression. He was obviously concerned about her but at a loss to know what to do now that the vivacious young woman he had been dating for the last three months had been replaced by this deeply upset girl who looked younger than usual.

Antoinette tried, but there was nothing she could do to stop the sobs and she was unable to get a word out.

'We can't go to the restaurant – you're in no state for it.' He frowned. 'We'd better go back to my place.'

She knew that he shared a flat with a friend, but they had never been there. If they weren't in a restaurant or at a dance, they were in his car. It was there they kissed and petted before he took her home. He had never tried to get any further with her than that, and Antoinette knew it was because he thought she was a girl he might get serious about. For a boy to take a girl that he respected to bed was tantamount to an engagement and they weren't ready for that yet, no matter what Antoinette's rosy daydreams were.

They drove to his flat and he took her inside. It was empty – his friend was out – and he led her gently to the settee and sat her down. She had stopped crying now but her breathing was still irregular and her body still shaking.

'I'll get you a drink,' said Derek kindly. 'You look like you need one this time.'

He poured her a stiff measure of whiskey, topped it up with cola and handed it to her. 'Drink that. It'll do you good.' He poured the same for himself, then sat down next to her and put his arm round her shoulders.

With shaking hands, she lifted the drink to her mouth and took a sip.

'That's better,' he said. 'Now, tell me what the problem is.'

She lifted a tearstained face to his. 'It's my father. He hit me.' The tears came back again, and she wiped them away with one hand and took a deep swallow of her drink.

From Derek's expression, it was clear he didn't know much about families where fathers hit their daughters. He had had a sheltered, middle-class upbringing and no one he knew rowed violently like that. 'Why did he hit you?'

'Because I told him the television was mine.'

'And?'

'He hit me in the breast.' Fresh tears flowed.

'Was your mother there?'

'Yes, and she did nothing as usual. She was in the kitchen and she didn't see where he hit me. It wouldn't have made any difference if she had.'

Derek frowned. 'He's hit you before?'

'Yes.'

'Look, answer me this – does your father ever hit your mother?'

'No.'

'Why not? If he's violent, why is it only with you?'

'Because she would leave him. She can control him when she wants.' And with that sentence, fresh sobs burst out of her.

Derek sat waiting for the new outburst to cease. He seemed confused and uncomfortable, fumbling for something to say. At last he said, 'Well, if he hits you, why do you stay there? You could leave home now, couldn't you? After all, you work and earn your own money. And now that your little dog has gone, there's nothing to keep you there, is there?'

The conversation was not going the way Antoinette had hoped.

Where is his offer of help, she thought desperately. When is he going to tell me that he'll take care of me and look after me?

All of a sudden, she wanted him to understand the serious nature of what had really happened. Surely then he would be completely outraged and that alone would make him want to take care of her.

'The look on his face when he hit me was the same as before he went to prison,' she said slowly.

'He's been in prison?' asked Derek, surprised. 'What for?'

'For making me pregnant,' she whispered. Immediately, she felt his body stiffen. He withdrew his arm from her shoulders and turned to face her.

'What did you say?' he asked in a low voice.

The look of stunned disbelief on his face that had suddenly grown pale made her want to take back her words but she knew it was too late. And without being able to retract them she found the story of her childhood pouring from her. She told him about the years of abuse she had suffered at the hands of her father. The only other times she had spoken of it was first to the police, once to a teacher and later to the psychiatrists. This was the first time she had ever confided in someone she cared about and who she believed cared for her.

But to her horror, she didn't see sympathy, understanding and compassion in Derek's eyes. Instead she saw repugnance as he realized that the unspoilt virgin he had fallen in love with was someone very different, someone who repulsed him with what had happened to her. She was no longer a pretty, amusing companion but someone sordid and ugly.

Looking at him through her tears, she saw and recognized the revulsion that she had seen so often in people's eyes when she was fourteen years old and the outside world learned what had happened to her. She heard the echo of her father's threats repeated time and again when she was a child: 'People won't love you if you tell, Antoinette. Everyone will blame you.'

In her imagination she saw the looks of disdain on people's faces as they turned away from her and slammed their doors. She saw the children she had been to school with forbidden to talk to her as though by acknowledging of her presence they too would be contaminated.

Why was I so stupid as to think anything would be different now, she thought miserably.

She felt that all she could do was try to gather the remnants of her dignity. She sat up straight and stiffened her back bone. There was no point in talking any more. She knew that she had taken a gamble and lost. 'Are you going to drive me home?' she asked.

'No. I'll call you a taxi and give you the money.' His face contorted with the effort of wanting to communicate something to her. She knew that he was by nature a kind boy but that he was a product of his upbringing. He believed that nice girls did not sleep around and that unwanted pregnancies resulted in marriage or disgrace. He had probably never heard of a girl having sex with her father, never knew that such a crime existed. She watched conflicting emotions pass over his face until finally he spoke.

'Look, you have to leave home. If I went to the police, your father could be arrested with his record but that wouldn't help you any. There's only one thing that can help you and that's to leave their house.'

She stared back at him. She was just as eager now for the conversation to end as he was.

He continued, 'You're going to work in Butlins in the next few weeks so don't go back.'

'If I do that, will you keep seeing me?' she said, unable to keep the imploring note out of her voice. But she knew the answer even as she asked.

'No.' He looked at her then and she could see clearly that his affection for her had died. 'I want to get married and have children and I could never marry you. Do you want to know what I think?'

She didn't but she knew he was going to tell her.

'When you meet someone again, don't tell them about your father. Don't tell anyone. Don't tell your friends and definitely don't tell men – not if you ever want to have another boyfriend, that is.'

They sat in stony silence until the taxi came. Antoinette did not want to be told that he never wanted to see her again. She just wanted to leave before the control over her facial muscles deserted her. Then she remembered how she had coped before, when she was just a girl of fourteen. Then she had separated her emotions, not allowing reality to penetrate her consciousness. That, she decided, was what she would have to do again.

Chapter Sixteen

Joe had not returned to the gate lodge the evening that his daughter was leaving home.

She knew that he would delay his return until some time after she had left. Her mother acted as though it was just another day and her daughter was leaving for a holiday. Antoinette tried to make herself believe that too. After all, she was going to work in a holiday camp so surely she would have some fun.

When her small suitcase was packed and everything was ready, Antoinette turned to face Ruth. She fought her need to throw herself into her mother's arms for one last hug; she knew that any show of regret on Ruth's part would be an act. Instead, she offered her cheek and received a cool kiss in return.

'Goodbye, darling. Don't forget to drop a postcard, will you?'

'No, of course not, Mummy,' she said, unable to break the deeply ingrained habit of obedience. Picking up her case, she opened the door and walked down the path to freedom.

It was not the first time she made the crossing between Northern Ireland and the mainland. She had been born in England and had only come to live in the country where her father was from when she was five and a half.

When the bus arrived at the docks and she saw the ship swaying gently in the oily water, she remembered the journey she and her mother had made eleven years ago when she was five and a half. With Judy, they had travelled from Kent to Liverpool by train and from there had taken the twelve-hour ferry crossing to Belfast. Her father had gone on ahead to find them a place to live and get himself a job, but he would be waiting for them at the docks.

Antoinette recalled the small chills of excitement that had sent shivers creeping up her spine when, far too small to be able to see over the boat's rails, she had to be lifted up. Then, in the early hours of a damp morning she had caught a glimpse of the Belfast docks. This, she was sure, heralded the first day of living in a country where they would all be happy.

A lump came into Antoinette's throat when, in her mind's eye, she saw her younger self wriggling with anticipation as she searched the crowds for a glimpse of her father. To her, in those days, he was just a big handsome man who made her mother laugh and bought his daughter presents.

To Ruth's delight, Joe had borrowed a car to meet his family at the docks so they could travel the final stage of the journey in comfort. Warmly wrapped in a tartan rug, their little girl had sat in the back seat craning her neck to take in everything about the new country they were going to live in. She had held Judy up to the window and excitedly pointed out the different scenery to her. Antoinette remembered wistfully the rapturous greeting her large Irish family had given them. They had all been waiting in her grandparents' tiny terrace house when Joe and his family arrived, ready to make a fuss of her and spoil her as much as they could. She was the first grandchild and the youngest member of the family and she had come to love her plump, white-haired Irish grandmother,

her taciturn grandfather, her aunts, uncles and her numerous cousins.

Then, when Antoinette was eleven, the family had moved back to Southern England, hoping to find the happiness that always seemed to elude them. By then the happy child that she had been when she arrived on the boat in Belfast had disappeared, replaced by a pale-faced, depressed and lonely eleven-year-old who had already been suffering at the hands of her father for five years. Antoinette had been unhappy in England and when, only three years later, she had been told that they were moving back to Ireland, she had been relieved.

The thirteen-year-old who had returned to Ireland was a pale shadow of the Antoinette who had arrived when she was little. Although she anticipated finishing her schooling there and going on to university, excitement had ceased long before to be an emotion she felt. By then her world had become a grey place and even the thought of seeing her family again did not lift the cloud of depression that hung over her. At thirteen she knew she was trapped in a life where she saw no escape and only Judy's presence gave her comfort. Since then, her life had descended further into misery and what felt like an endless punishment for things she had no power over.

Antoinette thrust away the thoughts that seeing the boat had conjured up; she wanted to forget her parents and her family's rejection. She wanted to push to the back of her mind the nagging worry that, apart from the temporary accommodation that Butlins provided during the summer, she was sixteen and a half and homeless.

I'm not going to think about that now, she told herself firmly. All that can wait until I get back. Right now, I'm going away on an adventure and that's all I'm going to concentrate on. I'm going to work all summer, earn my own money and, best of all, meet people who know nothing about me or where I come from.

She forced a cheerful smile on to her face as she climbed up the ramp that led onto the boat and made her way to the cabin she had reserved. She wanted time there alone. She was determined that Antoinette was going to be left behind on the Irish shore and that when the boat docked, it was Toni who was going to emerge.

Toni dressed in the height of fashion and wore a modish backcombed hairstyle. Her face was made up in the same way as other girls, with pale face and lips and heavy black eyeliner and mascara. Toni was a girl with a happy home, caring parents and a plan to take a secretarial course, and Toni was ready to meet new friends.

Once in the cabin, Antoinette began her transformation. She pulled off the clothes she had left home in. In the bottom of her case she placed the grey skirt and the hated blue twin set. She pulled on instead a pair of new snug-fitting jeans, a white shirt and a new pair of soft leather pumps. Standing on the only chair in the cabin, she admired her reflection in the tiny mirror above the wash basin then jumped down and reached for her make-up bag. It only took a few minutes for her to paint on the face of a bright confident teenager and hair hurriedly lacquered completed the look. Like a snake, she had shed her old skin and now she had metamorphosed into a typical teenager. She looked into the mirror again and saw a girl who was looking forward to the months ahead, one who had no worries and one who was going to be popular. She was suddenly full of optimism and hope.

Trying out her new image, she left the small cabin and went to the bar. She eyed the bottles of vodka longingly. Although she knew she easily looked eighteen, she was scared of being challenged, so she ordered a coffee instead. Taking it to a small table, she surveyed the other passengers sitting in groups and wondered if any of them were going to the same destination as she was.

The clanging of the gangway being lifted was followed by the shudder of the boat as it started leaving the dock. Antoinette looked out of the porthole and watched the skyline of Belfast fading into the distance as the huge vessel gradually left the docks until it vanished altogether. Not until the only light left was the dim silver glow of the moon casting shadows on the dark depths of the Irish Sea and glimmering on the white swell of the waves did she tear her eyes away. Then she went back to her cabin and went to sleep.

In the morning, she got up and dressed in her new incarnation. Then, clutching her case, she went to watch the boat entering the Liverpool docks.

Chapter Seventeen

She had all the directions written down on how to get to Butlins. First she had to catch a train to North Wales. There, coaches would be waiting to take her and the other recruits to the holiday camp.

The station in Liverpool was easy to find although, after Belfast, the city was huge and daunting. Once there, Antoinette quickly found her train and settled herself by a window. She had lied about her age to obtain her work at Butlins but after numerous peeks into the mirror and several repairs to her make-up, she convinced herself that nobody would guess she was eighteen months below the required age of eighteen. The train pulled out of the station and she quickly lost herself in a daydream as the scenery flashed by outside the window. It felt like no time at all before they arrived at the destination, and she alighted from the train and went to find the coach that would take her to the camp. It was parked near the station and it was filling up with summer recruits like herself. Scattering their luggage carelessly in the aisles, the girls chattered and laughed as they piled into every seat. Antoinette found herself a place and settled in, enjoying the holiday atmosphere on board. It didn't feel at all like workers on their way to their employment, more like an outing. Perhaps, she thought hopefully, this was going to be fun.

Butlins must be as large as Lisburn, Antoinette thought, as the coach finally drove through the gates. The holiday camp looked like a small town with streets lined with pubs, restaurants and shops, and behind them numerous rows of single-storey wooden chalets. Nearby were large dining halls. Everywhere she looked she could see groups of casually dressed holidaymakers wandering around.

Piling out of the coach, the new members of staff gathered up their luggage and then were led to their chalets. Antoinette was shown to her accommodation by a blue-coated member of staff who informed her that this was his third season. Blue coats belonged to the camp supervisors, he explained, and should new members of staff have any problems, it was to them that they could go.

Antoinette was to share with three other girls and, being the last to arrive, had been allotted a top bunk and a small locker for her belongings. This was to be her home for the next three months. She looked around the room and wondered briefly how four people could live side by side in it for the duration of the summer. Its four bunks covered by thin blankets took up most of the space, leaving scarcely any room for the coffee table and four wooden chairs. On a small cupboard there was a kettle, tea pot, milk jug and cups. Voices floated through walls hardly more than partitions on one side, while music came through the other.

The three girls whom she was to share with looked the opposite of what her mother would have described as 'nice girls'. Dressed in tight clothes, their faces heavily made up and cigarettes hanging out of the sides of their mouths, they sat painting their nails. They glanced up at her without much interest then showed her the small cupboard where she could hang her clothes.

One of them made a pot of strong tea. 'Would you like a cup?' she asked Antoinette as she placed the pot in the middle of the coffee table.

'Yes please,' Antoinette replied politely.

'Get yourself a cup then,' the girl said, nodding at the cupboard. Antoinette did as she was told.

They sat down, drinking their tea as the girls' nails dried, and started chatting.

'What's your name then?' asked one.

'I'm Toni,' she said, and they nodded, accepting this without question. They came from the North of England, they told her, and were old hands at Butlins – this was their fourth season.

'This is my first time,' confided Antoinette. 'I'm pretty nervous. I've no idea what it will be like.'

'Don't worry,' the youngest of the trio, a small bubbly brunette, told her. 'We'll show you the ropes all right. There's lots to do here.'

'And lots of men to do it with!' another of the group, a pretty bleach-blonde, said with a laugh.

They started to discuss their adventures with relish. Antoinette listened to them talk with what she hoped was a nonchalant expression on her face. One side of her wanted to feel part of this group of girls, all very different from ones she had known in Ireland, while the other part recoiled from their careless mention of boys.

Since breaking up with Derek, she had had no wish to meet anyone else. As she listened to the three women talking, it was becoming clear that things were quite different here. In

Ireland, there was a rigorous code of behaviour and young people did not expect to have sex – at least, not easily. That did not exist here. She heard the girls mention condoms as carelessly as she would have asked for a second spoon of sugar. Just hearing the word made her cringe and she felt her confidence, which had been increasing, begin to ebb.

Men of all different shapes and sizes came to Butlins in droves, her new room-mates informed her. With plenty of money in their pockets, they were out for a good time. Each of the girls had acquired a boyfriend at the start of the previous season but they'd already replaced that one several times over and would do so again a few more times before they returned home. When each new romance had lasted its fortnight and the holiday was over, there were tearful goodbyes and promises to write but that was all quickly forgotten when the next coach emptied out yet another group of eager young males.

'Don't you want a steady boyfriend?' Antoinette asked, thinking of the girls back home who wanted nothing else. As soon as the question had left her lips and three pairs of eyes looked blankly at her, she knew that she had given away the fact that she was a lot greener than she looked.

'Who wants to get stuck with one?' cried one of the girls. 'Not when every fortnight new ones with loads of cash arrive.'

They all whooped with laughter at Antoinette's face, which she could feel had turned scarlet, and their eyes sparkled at the expectation of the nights ahead of them. Antoinette had a sinking feeling that she was not going to enjoy herself as much as she had thought.

The pretty brunette saw her embarrassment and asked frankly, 'Are you a virgin, then?'

Antoinette nearly gasped aloud with horror. It was a question no nice Irish girl would have dreamt of asking or answering, come to that. She struggled with what to answer. To say 'no' would make her one of them, but then she would be expected to join in their activities. To say 'yes' would immediately make her different, something she did not want to be.

Her room-mates took pity on her. From her confusion and the pause while she tried to think of a reply, they assumed she had given herself away. She was obviously still a virgin – in their eyes, it was much more shaming to be inexperienced than it was to sleep with boys.

'Say, how old are you anyway?' one asked, looking at her closely.

She wondered for a minute whether to try and pretend she was eighteen but she knew immediately they wouldn't believe her. 'I'm sixteen and a half,' she said.

The girls looked at each other and then at Antoinette.

'You're taking a bit of a risk, aren't you?' said the brunette.

'I know. I lied about my age because I wanted to come here so badly. You won't tell, will you?'

'Don't worry about us – we won't breathe a word.'

'Do you promise?'

'Course we do. We don't mind how old you are,' said one, and the others nodded.

'But if you are that young, you had better hang on to it for a bit longer!' said the blonde kindly.

They asked her why she was there and Antoinette quickly made up a story of her father leaving her mother and there not being enough money to pay for her school fees. She had come, she said, to save as much as she could. She could tell that she now had their sympathy and that she had gone from being a strange girl with a posh accent to someone young and innocent who needed looking after.

'All men are bastards,' the trio chorused in unison.

'If any of them gives you bother you just come to us,' said the blonde and her two friends nodded in agreement.

Antoinette suddenly felt secure as she basked in the warmth of her new friends' unexpected kindness. That evening, the girls took her out with them and showed her where she could apply for extra evening work if she wanted it.

'Leave it till tomorrow,' one said.

'Wait till you've done a day's work and see how you feel,' advised another.

'Don't forget you want to have some fun as well,' added the third as they started on their pub crawl.

The bars were bigger than the dance halls in Belfast and packed with families. Here it seemed that three generations went on holiday together, as well as groups of friends of both sexes. The girls' first stop was a brightly lit bar with a large stage where a woman in a cotton dress belted out a Connie Francis number as a band played behind her. The bar staff were busy pulling pints of beer, pouring spirits into glasses and placing straws into bottles of fizzy drinks for the youngest customers. Waiters carrying trays of drinks fought their way through the throngs of happy, sun-kissed customers, young and old. Laughing children clutching bags of crisps chased one another through the legs of the adults, while teenage girls tossed their hair and gave sideways looks at the groups of youths, and honeymoon couples stood in pairs with their arms encircling each other.

Antoinette found to her relief that her room-mates had taken her under their wing and they explained everything she needed to know about working at Butlins. By the end of the evening, her spirits had lifted and they all returned happily to the chalet where Antoinette slept contentedly in her top bunk until her little alarm clock woke her at six thirty.

Unlike the older girls, Antoinette did not find rising early difficult and she further endeared herself to the group by making the morning tea. At seven fifteen, the trio took Antoinette to the huge dining rooms where hundreds of holidaymakers would be fed over two sittings. They left her with a supervisor to learn the ropes and went off about their own tasks. After a quick tour of the work place, she was given her uniform of a checked dress and she changed into it, preparing herself for the work ahead. She was confident that she could do the job easily, thankful that her time working in the coffee bar had prepared her for the work here. Unlike most of the other new girls who wore pretty kitten-heeled shoes, she knew what standing for several hours meant and had brought sensible shoes and cotton socks. She glanced with some pity at girls who were obviously wearing nylons, for she knew that by the end of the day they would have blisters on their heels.

Each waitress was allocated a station comprising ten tables and an area where cutlery was washed. In the course of two hours, eighty people had to be served, plates cleared and cutlery washed before the staff was fed. Using plate racks to stack the meals, the waitresses trotted up the aisles, almost throwing the dishes in front of the customers before rushing back to the huge heated trolleys to load up again. Back and forth they ran, dispensing as many meals and smiles as possible. Waitresses were very aware that wide smiles increased the amounts of tips given to them at the end of each week when, on departure, the holidaymakers showed their appreciation for the service they'd received.

There were three shifts a day, and after each one the staff hurriedly ate their own meals. No sooner was their last mouthful swallowed than it was time to lay the tables for the next sitting.

The evening was a repeat of lunchtime but with three courses to be served, which meant placing plates of food down in front of holidaymakers two hundred and forty times. The waitresses had an even greater interest in giving a quick service at dinner: they all wanted to return to their chalets and change for a night out. As soon as dusk fell, the staff at Butlins entered into the holiday spirit just as much as the guests did, and the neon lights of the numerous bars and clubs beckoned them to party the night away.

Antoinette had decided to take her new friends' advice and only work five nights a week and leave the other two for enjoyment. Her room-mates assured her that they would make sure that she was looked after.

'We'll stop any boys coming on to you heavy' was what they had actually said.

Feeling like the group's mascot but happy nevertheless, she was under the umbrella of their protection whenever she left the chalet with them for another night out.

Antoinette had put her name down for waitressing in the large bar they had been in on the first night. The manager had smiled at her as he asked the only question he seemed interested in hearing the answer to: how many nights did she want to work? And she was due to start there the next night. The families that frequented it were better tippers than teenagers, her friends had informed her. Youngsters tended to run out of money before their holiday was over and tips were important. If she could live on them, all her wages could be saved and she calculated that by the end of the season she should have enough money to pay for a bedsitter plus a term's fees at the college.

* * *

Life quickly fell into a routine at the camp. During the day, she worked hard waitressing the tables and serving the holiday-makers. In the evenings, she would make her way to the bar and start her shift there. The walls would shake as the bands turned up the volume on their speakers to stop the hum of conversation of hundreds of revellers drowning their music out completely. Whatever the age of the customer, they had one desire in common: to have a good time and enjoy their holiday, and that created an infectiously happy mood. Here, there was no room for sadness. Everybody wanted to have fun and to make the most of every minute. Antoinette found herself caught up in the atmosphere and her depression over Derek lifted. She pushed firmly thoughts of her parents and the uncertain future that awaited her at home to the back of her mind.

I'll deal with that later, she told herself. I like it here. I've made friends, I've got somewhere to stay, plenty of work to keep me busy and three months to enjoy myself, so I may as well make the most of it.

On her evenings off, she was determined to have fun. Entertainment at Butlins was free, not only for the holiday-makers but also for the staff as well. Every morning, the holi-daymakers were greeted with the words 'Good morning, campers!' broadcast through the loud speakers. Then a red-coated entertainer would announce the planned activities for the day. There was plenty for everyone, young or old, and Antoinette and her room mates would listen to the entire menu of what was on offer that evening before making their choice.

Antoinette's favourite were the talent nights when hope-ful performers would shed their daytime clothes, don their finest and strut on stage with all the confidence of a true professional. One of their fellow waitresses, who wore glasses as thick as the bottom of Coca-Cola bottles and shyly scurried up and down aisles serving tables, transformed herself at night into a glamorous club singer. Her checked cotton uniform was replaced by a sparkling dress, and instead of socks and plimsolls she wore four-inch heels, leaving her glasses backstage. When she opened with her rendering of 'Summertime', the room would fall silent and goosebumps rose on every arm as the silvery notes of her voice drifted into all four corners of the room. Holding the microphone in one pale hand while the other fell loosely to her side, she stood gazing myopically at an audience that was only a blur to her as she lost herself in the music of the famous Gershwin song. She received the thunderous applause afterwards with only a small puzzled smile, as though she did not believe in the power of her voice; then she would leave the stage and disappear. The next day she was the softly spoken, shy waitress again.

On other evenings, the four girls would go and see the usual entertainers – singers, dancers, comedians and magicians and every other kind of showman – all hoping that a talent scout would see them and lead them to stardom. Some went on to find fame, others sank into oblivion. Antoinette liked the magicians who found doves under handkerchiefs and gave the holidaymakers the illusion of sawing their skimpily dressed assistants in half, but they always emerged intact from their box, smiling at the crowd as the lights sparkled on their sequinned costumes.

To her delight, she found that on the five evenings she worked the holidaymakers were even more generous than she had expected. Every night she counted out the handfuls of silver change which they had left for her on their table. It meant that she was able not only to save all her wages but a good deal of her tips as well. Then, to add to what she thought of as her good luck, Butlins informed her that for every week she had worked she would receive a bonus of ten shillings, provided she stayed to the end of the season. Added to both her daytime and evening wages, that meant she had enough money not just for her rent and fees but to buy clothes suitable for a secretarial college.

Working both days and nights made the time pass so quickly that she hardly had time to miss home. She sent several postcards to her mother, keeping her up to date with her activities and letting her know that she was safe, but only received one short letter in reply.

A week before she left, Antoinette and her new friends went shopping for suitable clothes for the secretarial course she hoped she would be starting in the autumn. Before she left Ireland, she had registered herself but only when she returned would she know if she had been awarded a place. Antoinette wanted to look demure and ladylike and recalled how Derek's friend Charlotte had looked on that disastrous evening when they had met. She would copy that look, she decided, and picked out simple, elegant skirts and jumpers. Like three mother hens, the trio clucked their disapproval at the plain garments she chose. They favoured a bolder, more glamorous look and were vocal in expressing their opinion. With a wide smile, Antoinette ignored them and paid for her purchases. She was delighted with her choices, even if they were not, so she took them over the road to a café to celebrate with scones, cream cakes and cups of strong tea.

The final day at Butlins arrived. Antoinette was surprised at how emotional she felt leaving the place, and realized that she had been happy there. The work had been hard but she had also had lots of fun and made good friends. All the activity had made the time go by so fast that she could hardly believe she had been there three months. Everybody bustled about, packing their things and preparing to return to normal life.

'Will we see you next year?' asked one of her room mates.

'I hope so,' said Antoinette.

'You'll nearly be the right age anyway,' said another mischievously. 'We won't have to fight all the lads off for you then.'

Antoinette laughed. She'd enjoyed being their mascot and had felt safe all summer under her friends' protection. They all hugged and made arrangements to meet at the same place next year, before boarding their coaches that would take them to their different destinations.

As the coach to the station pulled away from the camp, Antoinette waved frantically to her girlfriends, before settling back into her seat. She didn't know what the coming year held for her and she was nervous about returning home. She would have to start making arrangements to live in her own place now, and cope with starting at the college. It was all rather daunting.

But I'll be back next year, if I possibly can, she promised herself. And I don't see why I shouldn't be.

Antoinette could not have known, that week in early September, that her life was about to change again. She would never return to work another season.

Chapter Eighteen

Antoinette sat on one of the wooden seats outside the inter-view room. In her bag she had a term's fee for the secre-tarial college. At last, after two years of saving added to what she had made during the Butlins season, she had enough money to realize her ambition. Now she wondered nervously if she would be accepted. She had already been provisionally accepted on the basis of her application form but it all rested on the personal interview with the principal, Miss Eliot.

She had started that day by brushing out her beehived hair for a more sober style and she applied her make-up sparingly. Then she put on one of the plain skirts and jumpers that she had bought in Wales, hoping that she had made the right choice. She wanted so badly to look the same as the other girls applying.

But there was one thing she didn't have that all the other applicants would have, and that was a parent in attendance. Well, there was nothing she could do about that. She would just have to go on her own.

Now, as she waited her turn for an interview, she was aware that she was attracting curious gazes from the other two people present: a girl about her own age and a woman who was obviously her mother. They were dressed in similar outfits of smart tailored coats with fur collars, and low-heeled polished shoes that matched the handbags they clasped in leather-gloved hands. They looked relaxed and comfortable and the girl seemed confident about the interview ahead. Antoinette watched them go as they were called in for their turn, wishing she had just an ounce of their self-confidence.

She was the last to be ushered in to the principal's office. As she entered she saw an imposing woman in her late fifties sitting behind a desk. She was dressed in a dark grey suit with her thick hair pulled away from her face into a severe bun and seemed an austere figure to Antoinette. Miss Eliot looked surprised and then displeased at the sight of the unaccompanied teenager.

'You're Antoinette Maguire, aren't you? Are you alone?' she asked abruptly.

'Yes.' There was no point in trying to make excuses so she said nothing more.

Miss Eliot gave her a curious look. 'Well, it is usual in these circumstances for a parent to be present. If you are offered a place, I shall need to discuss the matter of our fees with someone.'

Antoinette knew that there was a waiting list of girls wanting to enter the prestigious college. From the expression of disapproval on Miss Eliot's face, she had the sinking feeling that the absence of a parent was going to count against her more than she had thought. But she had not spent two years working and saving to admit defeat easily.

She straightened her back, looked Miss Eliot in the eye and said, 'I've got the fees in my handbag. I've been saving them up for the last two years.'

For a moment, the older woman looked completely nonplussed, then her expression of disapproval softened. 'Do you want to be a secretary so badly, my dear?'

Antoinette thought that truth might win the day. 'No,' she said frankly, 'it's that I want a school-leaving certificate stating that I left school at eighteen not fourteen, which I did.' She saw no point in adorning the facts when she was sure that Miss Eliot would see straight through any subterfuge.

Miss Eliot allowed herself a brief smile at the teenager's bravado. 'Sit down, please.'

Antoinette sat with relief. She knew that she had passed some sort of test and the rest of the interview passed quickly and easily. It seemed like only a few minutes later that Miss Eliot asked her to sign the forms and pay her deposit. Then, with a brief handshake, the principal welcomed her as a student of the Belfast Secretarial College.

Antoinette had received a distinctly frosty welcome on her return home from Butlins. Her father ignored her, spending even more time than usual out of the house and her mother was cool, only speaking to her to urge her to find her own place to live.

'You know what was agreed, Antoinette,' she said. 'You're to move out. Your father doesn't want you here any longer. You're perfectly able to support yourself now.'

As soon as she had her place at the college, Antoinette went looking for somewhere to live. Before then, she would have had difficulty finding someone who would rent a room to her but now that she could prove that she was a student and explain that she needed to rent rooms near her college, landladies would be more amenable. Almost at once she found somewhere she thought would be suitable – a bedsitter in a shared house in the student area of the Malone Road. It wasn't the most salubrious place she could imagine, but it was cheap, the landlady was prepared to rent to her, and it would be an escape from the home where she was so clearly no longer wanted.

She put down her deposit and said she could move in immediately. Then she went back to pack her things. Her parents were both out, so she left the gate lodge alone and with no goodbyes.

I ought to feel sad, she thought as she climbed down the stairs holding her suitcase. But she felt nothing. After all, Judy was no longer here to provide some vestige of warmth and companionship. There was nothing here for her anymore.

She shut the door behind her, believing that she would never return.

On the first day of term, Antoinette woke early. She looked around her dismal bedsitter with its thin carpeting where the pattern had faded so much it was nearly indistinguishable. It was sparsely furnished, with two scratched wooden chairs at an equally worn table and an old armchair by the window. She had bought some brightly covered cushions to make it more comfortable but despite her brave attempts to make the room cosier, it still looked bleak. But she knew that she was lucky to have found a place to live. Plenty of landladies would have refused to rent to young girls without work, even if she was a student. But a large deposit had secured the seedy room for her.

This was the first day of college; today, she would begin the training that would take her away from rooms like this one to a new life.

She stretched, then clambered off the sagging mattress and stumbled sleepily out into the passage that led to the communal kitchen. She had taken her bath the night before so that she would not have to queue for the bathroom in the morning with the five other tenants who shared the house. All the others had been out the previous evening and she had been able to stoke the meter with plenty of coins and then soak in the enamel bath for as long as she wanted without fear of interruption.

In the kitchen, her nose wrinkled with distaste at the sight of the mess the other tenants had left: dirty plates were piled high in the sink and congealed food, remnants of a hasty supper, was stuck in hard lumps to the Formica kitchen table. She looked in vain for a clean cup and then, with a sigh, removed one from the scummy water in the sink and rinsed it under the tap. Setting the kettle to boil and putting some bread in the toaster, she waited for her breakfast and felt a pang of nostalgia for the gate lodge.

'But that was the life before *he* returned,' she told herself sternly. 'I'm better off here.' When she had made her tea and buttered her toast, she took her breakfast to her room. Once she'd finished, she dressed and then picked up her new case that contained all the books she needed for the course.

It would only take her half an hour to walk to the college and, mindful of having to economize, she decided to do just that. It was a pleasant early autumn day and as she crossed Belfast, her spirits lifted. She finally felt like the student she had wanted to be for so long.

Antoinette's fingers moved clumsily over the letters and knocked onto the black metal guard that prevented her from seeing the keyboard.

Concentrate, she told herself as she looked at the exercise book and placed her fingers over the correct keys. 'A, S, D, F,' she muttered, and then shifted her fingers across on to G, H, J, K, then L. She sighed. Surely people did not torture themselves daily on these machines? How would she ever learn to do it correctly? It seemed impossible, she thought as she repeated the frustrating exercise again.

'Concentrate, Antoinette,' said Miss Eliot in steely tones as she marched up and down between the desks, surveying each girl's efforts. 'Accuracy, not speed, is the purpose of this lesson,' she repeated for the umpteenth time.

The squat little typewriter with its matching guard seemed to mock her as her fingers searched for a rhythm. Forty-five more minutes passed. Outside the sun shone and inside twenty heads neatly coiffeured, not a beehive to be seen, bent to their task. Thirty-eight hands moved rhythmically but the two belonging to Antoinette felt as though their fingers had swollen during the night. Somehow they had become unmanageable appendages that slid off the keys and refused to obey her.

At last typing was over. A shorthand lesson followed and as she opened her book, Antoinette looked in dismay at what appeared to be numerous meaningless squiggles.

'How can I ever learn to write that?' she asked herself despairingly, as she tried to master Mr Pitman's peculiar slanting letters with their dots and hoops. She knew they had to be mastered. She needed a certificate stating she was qualified in shorthand to give her entry to the work place and she was determined that the next time she searched for employment, she would be armed with exam results. No more waitressing for her.

At the end of the first lesson, she felt she could start a letter *Dear Mr Smith …* but how she was ever going to finish it was a mystery.

The last lesson before lunch was bookkeeping and she was able to relax. All the practice in the coffee shop where she had to work out bills in her head had made numbers easy. She noticed to her satisfaction that she appeared to be the only one that thought so but she quelled her desire to smile. She did not want to draw any attention to herself or have to explain where her ability in mental arithmetic came from. Years of waitressing and adding up countless bills in her head might be the honest answer but it was not one she wanted to give.

The welcome lunch break came. Seeing the other girls meet in groups to make their arrangements, Antoinette picked up a book and quickly left for the nearest café. She did not want to try and mix with the other students. She would only have to answer awkward questions that she would rather avoid. Her circumstances and the fact that she lived alone in a bedsitter would be outside the comprehension of the other girls there. She knew what their homes would be like: there would be silver on the sideboards, thick rugs on the floors and glowing fires in the grates; their houses would smell of polish and the scent of flowers and, come the evening, aromas of cooking would waft from the kitchen.

Unlike Antoinette, these girls would not be concerned with the cost of food, or how many coins were put aside for the meters or whether they could pay the rent. Certainly none of them walked to the college to save fares. No, they were dropped off in the morning by mothers driving the family car and when they came home, they were greeted by loving parents who were interested in their progress.

She knew the kind of homes these girls came from. On her nocturnal walks taken to escape the claustrophobic loneliness of her bedsitter, she would wander through the middle-class suburbs of Belfast and pass houses where people like her class-mates lived. Through the large picture windows, she caught glimpses of families sitting together talking, or saw soft lights casting a glow on groups at the dining table engrossed in the evening meal and each other.

The girls who came from those homes all had that gloss that a worry-free life bestows. She recognized the confidence that protected them. Their lives were already planned – for the boys, university followed by a well-paid career; for their sisters, a genteel job that would not be too taxing before they got married and made caring for a family their priority.

As she ate her lunch in a nearby café, she thought of her cheerless temporary home: the communal kitchen with its constant mound of unwashed dishes, the lavatory where she had to take her own roll of paper each time she went, and the shared bathroom with its chipped bath. She pictured the waist-high scummy ring left by tenants too busy for such a mundane task as cleaning it. There was a hollowness inside her when she visualized the emptiness of her room and how bare it felt without even her dog to greet her. A wave of lone-liness threatened to choke her.

She pushed that feeling away and replaced it with another picture. It was of herself, well groomed with gleaming hair and beautiful manicured nails taking dictation in a modern office from a handsome male employer. She saw herself walking away, her notebook in hand, to sit in front of a shiny modern typewriter that ran on electricity and had no guard to hide its keys. She saw her hands move rapidly as she typed a letter without one spelling mistake, gave it to her employer ready for signature and heard him say with a grateful smile, 'I don't know how this company would manage without you.'

That daydream lasted through a second cup of coffee and still floated in her head as she made her way back to the college.

The end of term came and with it, the first set of exams. Antoinette had found the course monotonous and had already made up her mind to leave and find work. She may not have finished the entire year but she would have a certificate stating she had left the secretarial college at seventeen, was proficient in typing and basic bookkeeping and that her shorthand was passable. That would be enough to get her a job interview, she thought. She was desperate to start work, get an income and leave her bedsitter. The loneliness there felt as though it was killing her. She hadn't made any friends on her course and she hadn't tried to. Keeping separate felt like a necessity. She tried to keep it all inside and concentrate just on the future which must surely be brighter.

At the end of term, she passed her exams and left the college for good. She didn't regret leaving even though going there had been her dream for so long; she had got what she needed. Armed with her secretarial credentials and a personal reference from Miss Eliot, she went looking for a job and quickly found work as a receptionist at a small firm of hairdressers.

The work was not difficult and it was a friendly enough place. The girls who worked there were not like the middle-class lady-like types at the college; they were more like the ones she had gone to the dances with; but there was one difference when it came to making friends with them. When she had gone dancing, she had the confidence boost of several fortifying drinks but she couldn't do that in daytime and without the artificial bravado that alcohol provided, her confidence drained away. It was impossible to join in the light-hearted banter of the stylists. As a result, they thought she was aloof and after a few attempts at being friendly, they ignored her.

In a perverse way, that was what she wanted. While she yearned for the friendship of other young people, she was petrified of allowing anyone to become close. Her colleagues might tolerate or even like the girl she pretended to be, the one who had just left secretarial college and who talked with a middle-class accent. They would shun her completely if they discovered her past. Everyone assumed that she lived at home and she had no intention of them ever knowing the reality of her living arrangements. But she couldn't get out of the bedsitter until she had more money and replenished her savings, which had been almost used up by the cost of her course and supporting herself without working.

Until then, she would continue to keep herself to herself, and bear the loneliness as best she could.

Chapter Nineteen

Antoinette did not want to open her eyes again. One attempt earlier had been enough to tell her that daylight was going to hurt them but the need to go to the toilet had become a pressing one. Reluctantly she swung her legs out of the bed and shakily placed her feet on the cold lino that covered her small bedsitting-room floor. As she stood, the room spun and she had to place her hands on the wall to steady herself. She lurched to the door and then staggered into the cold passageway.

With legs that had become heavy during the night, she shakily took the few steps to the communal bathroom and looked at her reflection in the mirror. A pale face looked back at her, the only colour two bright red spots staining both cheeks. Her throat hurt, her head pounded while her whole body ached.

She knew she was suffering from a bad bout of 'flu and felt tears prickle as she thought longingly of her bedroom at the gate lodge. A year before, when she had succumbed to a similar attack, her mother had brought cups of tea and sympathy to her room, along with cool drinks and tasty snacks designed to tempt her appetite. As she thought about it, Antoinette could almost feel the comforting sensation of her mother's hands tenderly brushing her hair, damp with perspiration, back off her face. When Ruth had returned from work in the evenings, she had plumped up Antoinette's pillows and cooked her supper to eat on a tray on her knees. When she had finished, she would snuggle down to sleep and Ruth would gently draw up the soft wool blankets around her shoulders.

That was the time before *he* had returned. That was the time when Ruth had been able to show the maternal love for Antoinette that her daughter craved. It had seemed as though Antoinette's illness had made her feel needed when her daughter was helpless and had brought out an affection that she rarely allowed to surface. Antoinette had basked in it, smiling up gratefully at her mother from her warm bed. The child she had been so recently reappeared for the duration of her sickness and she had wanted to hold on to her mother's hand as she had done ten years before. But instead, she kept her fingers on the inside of the blankets, curling them tightly shut as she hid that need.

As she remembered, Antoinette felt an overwhelming longing to be there and to feel loved and looked after again.

Mummy would put me in my old bed, she thought. She would let me sleep and bring me cups of tea and heat up tins of tomato soup and serve it with thinly sliced bread and butter. It was invalid food which would soon make her feel better. Then later, when she was well enough to venture downstairs but not well enough to leave the house, she would wrap herself in her old pink candlewick dressing gown and sit in front of the fire. There, with her feet on the small round padded stool, she could watch her favourite programmes on the black and white television.

She was overwhelmed by the need to see her mother and be cosseted as she had been before. Just thinking of what it would feel like being at the gate lodge surrendering to Ruth's ministrations again made her feel better. She completely blocked from her mind the picture of her father, his anger at her and his jealousy at any attention her mother gave her.

Could I go back, she wondered. Just this once?

She had ventured back only once or twice since she had moved to the bedsitter and then only when she was sure her father would be out. She had her parents' work timetables written down in a small notebook and went home when she was certain of finding her mother there alone. Then, her mother had seemed pleased to see her and had even given her small packages of food to take back to the bedsitter.

Knowing that this was a morning that Ruth would be at home and her father at work, she pushed aside any lingering doubts she had. The great need to retreat back into childhood when her mother had made everything better decided her. She would go home.

Antoinette hurriedly dressed, threw her pyjamas and a change of underwear into a bag and still burning with fever walked to the bus stop. On the short journey home, she dozed until the bus delivered her almost to the doorstep. Clasping her small case in her hand, she walked unsteadily to the front door of the gate lodge, then remembered that she no longer had a key. She'd left it behind the day she went to Butlins, as her parents had requested. She knocked on the door then leant against the wall as dizziness threatened to overpower her.

She heard footsteps then the noise of the key being turned. The door swung open and her mother stood in the hall facing her. A worried smile failed to reach her eyes.

'Darling, what a nice surprise. Why aren't you at work?'

'I'm not well.' As the words left her, helpless tears filled her eyes and overflowed down her flushed cheeks.

'Come inside, dear, quickly.' Her mother ushered her in away from the prying eyes of any neighbour. With her fear of gossip and need to keep up appearances, Ruth certainly didn't want anyone wondering what Antoinette was doing crying on the doorstep. They went in to the hall and Ruth shut the door.

'I need to lie down. Please can I go to my bedroom?' As the words tumbled out, she felt her mother's hesitation.

Ruth's voice softened as she asked, 'Antoinette, whatever's wrong with you?' She touched her daughter's forehead briefly. 'Well, you're certainly burning up. All right, dear, your bed is still made up. Just get into it and I'll bring you up a cup of tea.'

With those words Antoinette felt cared for and protected for the first time in months. No sooner had she climbed into her old bed then her mother appeared, drew the curtains shut, placed the tea by her bed and gently kissed the top of her head. 'I've rung work to say I'll be in late,' she said. 'Now you get some rest.'

As soon as the door closed behind her, Antoinette fell into a fitful sleep. When she awoke a few hours later, she did not know where she was for a couple of moments. Disoriented, she stared into the gloom then realized she was back in her bedroom at the gate lodge. Something had woken her and she raised herself on to the pillows. The sound of raised voices filtered through her window – it was that which had disturbed her. She recognized the harsh pitch of her father's voice and the anger in it frightened her. She couldn't distinguish what was being said but she knew that her father was furious and that she was the cause. Her mother's softer tones suggested that she was trying to placate him.

Why are they outside, wondered Antoinette, puzzled. Her mother's distaste of showing any discord in public had always ruled out any disagreement outside the house.

As she had done so often when she was a small child, Antoinette slid down the bed and pulled the blankets over her ears. If she could not hear them maybe they would go away. Nevertheless, she could hear the creak of the stairs followed by the muffled sound of her mother's footsteps as she entered the bedroom. Instinct made Antoinette feign sleep. Her mother's hand touched her shoulder lightly, then she heard the words she had been dreading.

'Are you awake? You have to get up. Your father says you have to leave.'

Groggily, Antoinette opened her eyes and looked into her mother's face, searching for some reassurance that for once she was not going to obey her husband. A flash of guilt crossed Ruth's face, quickly replaced by a steely resolve.

'He's refusing to come into the house until you've gone. He says you've left home now and you can't just come back when it suits you. You have to stand on your own two feet.'

Instead of her usual condescending tones, Ruth's voice held a note of pleading.

Antoinette looked for the solicitude that she had seen earlier in her mother's face, hoping to see some softness in her expression that hinted she might relent. But there was no trace of Ruth's earlier concern and in its place was an expression of long suffering. Once again, Ruth had become the woman who never took responsibility for anything, but who placed the blame for all her misfortunes squarely on another's shoulders. This time, her expression said clearly that it was Antoinette's fault.

Too ill to fight her mother, or even to react, Antoinette hauled herself out of bed, dressed and picked up her bag.

Over the years when she tried to remember that night she couldn't. She only remembered that she left.

Chapter Twenty

First came the headaches.

In the early hours of the morning, the pain woke her. Her head felt as though it was clasped by a giant hand. She visualized the fingers pressing through her scalp, gripping her neck and then squeezing until the pain settled behind her eyes, distorting her vision.

During the day, when the headaches had passed, she felt lethargic, her limbs became heavy and her brain slowed until it felt sluggish. Her concentration faded and the print in books, which once had given her comfort, became blurred until even the short stories in magazines became too much for her, and she put them wearily aside.

Back at home in the bedsitter and trying to sleep, she found that there was no rest to be had. Her anxiety, her loneliness and her guilt poisoned her dreams, turning her nights into torment. She was deprived of rest; instead she was swept to dark places where demons chased her.

Sometimes she would have the sensation of falling and through her nightmare she felt her body twitch with the effort of trying to stop it. When she woke she would feel her heart pounding with lingering panic. Sudden sounds startled her and an overwhelming loneliness filled her mind.

Then the dream came; it came every night and it was so much worse than all the others that she would force herself awake. Then she would wait for daylight, determined to keep sleep at bay, terrified that if she closed her eyes it would return. The nightmare took her into a forest where tall trees grew so densely their foliage hid the sky and obliterated the light of the moon. Desperately, she searched for the way out as wet branches whipped her face and slimy tendrils curled snakelike round her legs and feet, hindering her frantic progress. The sense of being trapped was terrifying and it seemed that there were creatures hidden in the dense undergrowth. She felt animosity radiating from them as unseen eyes spied on her and somehow she knew her father was there amongst them. She could sense his shadowy presence watching and mocking her feeble attempts of escape.

Unable to see in the cold blackness of the forest, she only knew that she was terrified and lost. Then suddenly a gaping chasm would appear under her feet and she would feel herself begin to fall, sucked down by a force stronger than her willpower. She tried to touch the sides of the cavern and stop herself falling but her hands only grasped dank emptiness. Out of control, she fell blindly through the depths towards something unspeakable.

She knew she was asleep and would desperately fight to regain consciousness but not before a silent scream tore from her throat as she tumbled headfirst into darkness. Helpless mewing sounds escaped her mouth as panic broke through and released her. She would wake, sweating and breathless, still anxious and fearful as the nightmare faded. She knew that she had avoided hitting the bottom of the awful pit by seconds. Around her, the bedclothes were tangled where she had thrashed in her bed, her arms flailing.

Awake, she could not rationalize her premonition that something disastrous was about to happen, and was overcome by despair that she was still alive. Holding her wrists close to her face, she looked at the scars from two years before. Night after night, she would gaze at the fine blue lines that lay just below the surface of the skin and picture a razor slicing through them again.

She thought of swallowing a hundred aspirin as she had before, and then remembered the sickness that had racked her body hours after the stomach pump had been removed. She tasted again the bile that had burnt her throat.

If she managed to sleep again after her nightmare, then she woke at 4.30 exactly. It was as though a malicious spirit had set an alarm to rouse her. It was too early to get up, so she would curl up tighter and try to force herself to stay awake and keep her dreams at bay. As she dozed, images of the parents that no longer wanted her crept into her mind. Then she thought of her large Irish family that had scorned her and the people of her home town who had rejected her. She tried to push away thoughts of Derek and how repulsed he had been when he had realized who she really was. It seemed to her that Derek represented how people felt when the reality of her past was presented to them.

Antoinette's world began to shrink.

She could no longer function enough to go to work and she rang in to say she was sick. She thought she must be ill, though she had no idea what was wrong with her. All she knew was that the world had become a frightening place.

When she ventured out, the noise of the traffic hurt her head and she wanted to place her hands protectively over her ears to block it out. Crossing the road made her shake; every car seemed intent on her destruction and she was certain that they wanted to drive into her, run her over and maim her. Waves of panic made her legs tremble so severely that they almost refused to obey her as she hovered at the kerb. Each step across to the opposite side was an act of tremendous will.

Entering a shop was terrifying, for she saw animosity on every face. If other shoppers were silent, she knew it was because they had only just stopped talking about her. Unable to meet the eyes of shopkeepers, she would mutter her order and hurry out, clutching her goods tightly. She was sure that she was the cause of any laughter and the reason it turned into jeers that followed her out of the shop and chased her down the street.

When she got back to the house, she would creep up the stairs praying that the doors of the other tenants' rooms would remain closed. She could hear more whispering coming from behind the doors and she shut herself away in the sanctuary of her room, far from the malevolent voices. When she had to leave it, she would rest her head against the door and listen for sounds of life in the house. Running water, the flush of the toilet and the creak of the stairs or soft footsteps all warned her it was unsafe to go out. Only when she was reassured that there was no one about would she summon up her courage to leave.

At weekends she would hear laughter on the stairs, the sound of doors opening and blaring music which invaded her peace. She placed her fingers in her ears as she tried to block out the unwelcome sounds that crept under her door and into her room. Gradually, her world narrowed even further and she barely left the house. There was no question now of her returning to work but she wasn't well enough to worry about how she was to pay the rent. There were still some savings left and what she would do when they ran out was not a thought that she was able to dwell on. Antoinette had become completely isolated, cast adrift with no direction, and her only escape from the unrelenting depression was the sips she took from her secreted vodka bottle. It was her last remaining solace.

The game of happy families that Ruth had orchestrated for so many years had come to an end. Antoinette simply could not play her part any longer. She could not join in her mother's fantasy that they were a normal family and the comfortable lie that she was loved and needed like any ordinary daughter no longer had any power. From the night that her mother had thrown her out, sick and alone, the truth with its harsh facts had finally penetrated her defences and she was unable to deal with it. Now her mind had been invaded by a dark melancholia as she realized that throughout her life she had been fed a constant diet of deceit and despair.

Why couldn't she feel glad that her parents no longer expected her to be a part of their lives? Wasn't she free of them now? But Antoinette had been too controlled to learn independence. A dog that has been beaten for years will die if it is thrown out in the street to fend for itself. It will cringe in corners, not trusting a soul but always hoping for some kindness. The one emotion it will not feel is relief at its freedom.

Antoinette was incapable of seeking help; she was too ill to realize she needed it. Now the boxes inside her mind where she had locked away her memories had sprung open, spilling out the truth of her short life. All around her she could hear the whispers: they blamed and mocked her, said that nobody loved her, and that nobody ever would. They told her to disappear.

Petrified of re-entering her nightmares, she tried to avoid sleep and instead lay huddled up in bed, her eyes darting around the lighted room, searching the shadows for threats until she could no longer fight her overwhelming tiredness. At dawn, when she woke, the bird song that welcomed the day became a harsh sound which resounded in her brain. She would lay silent, clutching the blankets, her body shaking, while the tears that never seemed far away slid down her cheeks.

Then, the morning came when even leaving her bed took too much effort. She curled up tightly, her thumb entered her mouth, whimpers shook her and the ability to move deserted her.

Disembodied voices were in her room; they swirled above her head and floated in the air. She knew if she kept her eyes closed and stopped herself seeing who they belonged to, they would disappear. The words took shape and forced their way into her mind but still she tried to shut them out.

'Open your eyes, Antoinette. Can you hear me?'

She recognized the tones of her landlady but she curled up even tighter, not wanting to be disturbed. She heard footsteps as her landlady retreated. It seemed to her that only a very short time had passed when the voices returned.

'What's wrong with her, doctor? I can't wake her.'

Then another voice spoke. 'Antoinette, I'm a doctor. We're here to help you. There's nothing to be afraid of. We're here to help you,' he repeated gently.

Still she took no notice. She felt a hand on her face and fingers raised her eyelids.

She saw faces – the faces of her enemies staring down at her. Antoinette screamed and kept screaming.

For an instant she felt a sharp sting as a needle slid into her arm. Then, within seconds, she felt no more.

Chapter Twenty-One

Try as I might, I could not make those memories leave me. As I sat with the light fading I could sense my father's intimidating presence in the room with me, the man who all his life had relied on coercion, never logic or reasoning.

Only that morning, the day after he had died, I had arrived here at his house, a small whitewashed terrace in the centre of Larne. He had moved there shortly after my mother's death. To my dismay, he had sold the home that they had shared together and that she had cherished so much within only a few weeks of her dying.

Unlocking the door, I had stepped into a small windowless entrance hall. The stairs with their faded dark carpeting faced me but I did not want to tackle those upstairs rooms. Instead, I opened the door that led into the sitting room.

A small two-seater settee covered in dull burgundy with worn arms and springs that were trying to make their escape through the scuffed base had been placed opposite a large television. What, I wondered, had he done with the settee my mother had so painstakingly covered with pretty chintz material? Even the many cushions, covered with pastel fabric, which she had artfully scattered over each seating place, had disappeared. The mantelpiece held a cheap clock and instead of the delicate blue and white Dresden figurines which my mother had loved, the only ornament was a shiny china tabby cat which had the country of its origin stamped on its base in an unrecognizable alphabet.

The coal fire had been replaced by a modern ugly gas stove and in the recess by the chimney breast wooden shelves housed not the books my mother would have favoured but Joe's collection of dance trophies. Propped incongruously against their shiny, dust-free gilt was a small photograph. It was the picture of Antoinette aged three wearing a gingham dress which her mother had made all those years ago. He had removed it from its silver frame, letting the edges curl. I took it and placed it in my wallet.

I was relieved that this small charmless house held so few memories for me. Although I had visited once before, I had not noticed then how very little of my father's life with my mother remained. There was not even one photograph of her on display. It was as though with her death, her memory had been erased from his mind.

Wanting to rid the house of the stale smell that hung in the air, I opened the windows regardless of the chill that entered. I lit a cigarette and inhaled as deeply as I could, wanting that familiar tobacco smell to eclipse that oppressive odour of the house.

His presence was everywhere: worn carpet slippers sat by the side of an armchair that had become shiny with wear and the back showed a round greasy spot where his head had rested. An ashtray placed on the coffee table in honour of my only visit a few months before still remained there. He had managed to conquer his addiction to cigarettes when he had turned sixty. Mine had started once I had left my parents' home.

I wondered what the ashtray meant. Had my father hoped that I had been so forgiving that my visit would repeated? Did he really think that he had done so little wrong that it was only my selfishness that kept me in England? Was he able to fool himself to that extent? These were questions that I had no answer to and I would never be able to ask him myself now, so I mentally shrugged my shoulders. It was many years since I had tried to fathom the workings of my father's mind.

In the kitchen, a single cup and saucer sat on the draining board and a freshly ironed cream shirt carefully placed on a wire hanger was suspended on a hook by the kitchen door, as though my father would be coming back to put it on at any moment.

My parents' animals – a big, good-natured golden Labrador and two cats – had died several years before my mother's death and somehow their absence added to the house's desolate air. I remembered the love both my mother and father had lavished on them and again pushed aside the question: if they were capable of feeling love and even compassion for four-legged creatures, why had they felt so little for me?

Outside the back door, I glanced at the unkempt garden then turned away, almost tripping over my father's golf clubs. I felt the black cloud of depression settling on my shoulders again and firmly pushed it away.

'For God's sake, Toni,' I told myself impatiently. 'He's gone now. Just get on with sorting his papers and you can go back to England.'

I made myself put on the kettle to make a large mug of tea, but not before I scalded the mug with boiling water. I did not want to place my lips where his had been. Then I gathered my strength and turned to the job I had come here to do.

* * *

It was the first task that I found the most difficult. I found a notebook where my mother had kept her household accounts in a desk drawer. Meticulously filled in with her small neat handwriting, it showed a daily record of a frugal existence. Beside them were the bank statements. My father had been a thrifty man and had spent very little of what he had. The accounts showed a bigger sum in them than I had expected. Another statement showed that as well as his monthly pension, several substantial amounts had been paid in. One was from the sale of the larger house my parents had owned and the others from the sale of all the antiques my mother had painstakingly collected during her marriage. Found at junk shops and markets at bargain prices, her collection of china and ornaments had been cherished and displayed with pride. On the occasions I had visited, she always had a freshly acquired small item of beauty that she proudly showed me.

My mother had loved two things in her life – her garden and her antiques. They were all that gave her some happiness. Both had been done away with and forgotten in this old man's bare house.

It had not taken him long to erase her from his existence. The day after she died, when I had sat with her in the hospice until she finally passed away, I drove to the house where my parents lived. For the sake of her memory, I was prepared to suppress the rage I felt towards my father: the night she died he had refused to come to the hospice for that final goodbye and while I had sat holding her hand over that long lonely night, the man she had loved for so many years had preferred to drink at the British Legion club.

But, great as my fury was towards him and as much as I resented his absence that night, I still wanted the company of another person who had known and loved her. I wanted to walk in the garden she had created, look one last time at her collection of ornaments and feel her presence. I wanted to remember her as the mother she had been until I had turned six: the one who had played with me, read bedtime stories and let me crawl onto her lap for cuddles. That was the mother I had always loved. The other mother – the one who had sacrificed her child to live out her fantasy of a happy marriage and who never admitted her guilt – I would forget for now.

Arriving at the farmhouse my parents had converted some years previously, I was prepared to put aside my anger and drink a cup of tea with my father. I needed so much to delay the acceptance of her death and to share some memories with him, like any daughter should be able to do. I walked to the blue-painted front door and tried to push it open as I called for him. It was locked. I realized then that if I had hoped for any normality I was going to be disappointed.

Seizing the brass door knocker, I knocked as loudly as I could, then stepped back and waited for him to open the door.

I heard the shuffle of his footsteps then the turning of the key. As the door opened my father stood in the entrance barring my way, refusing to let me in. Instead, he glared at me with blood-shot eyes sunken into a face made puffy not with grief but, I knew by the smell of his breath, the excess of alcohol.

'What do you want?' he demanded. A flash of childhood fear made me recoil from him and I tried to hide it, but it was too late. He had recognized it and a gleam of triumph flashed into his eyes. 'Well, Antoinette? I asked you a question.'

Even from my father, a man who was supposed to be grieving, that degree of aggression took me by surprise but I managed to stand my ground. 'I've come to see if you are all right and if you need any help sorting out my mother's things. I thought while I was here we'd have a cup of tea.'

'Wait here.' With that, he slammed the door in my face, leaving me staring at it aghast.

Surely he would want to discuss the funeral arrangements, I thought. I'm their only child.

He didn't.

After a few minutes had passed, the door opened and he thrust several bulging black rubbish sacks at me.

'Here are your mother's things,' he announced. 'You can take them to a charity shop. Oh, and don't be taking them to one nearby as I wouldn't want anyone to recognize anything.'

And with those words he slammed the door shut again, I heard the key turn and I was left standing on the doorstep with my mother's clothes bursting out of plastic sacks that lay in a heap by my feet.

He hasn't even wasted one of her suitcases, I thought disbelievingly, as I packed them into my car.

It was not until after my mother's funeral that I discovered that he had stealthily been selling her possessions before she died, something he would not have wanted me to be aware of and probably why he didn't allow me into the house where I would have seen for myself how much was already gone. While he did not care for my opinion, he would not have wanted that deed to be talked about.

Now, as I looked at the bank statements, I saw that he had not sold them out of necessity but out of sheer greed. All he wanted was to see that money in his accounts. Judging by the many creases in the statements, he had satisfied his avarice often.

Surely, I thought, he must have known that my mother would have wanted me to have some of her collection as a memento, even if it was only one of the pieces I had bought her. I simply did not believe that when she knew she was dying, she had left no instructions to that effect.

The walls of the house felt as though they were closing in on me as I felt again the effects of my father's spite.

I remembered then the conversation between us when I had learnt that their house had been put on the market before her death and that within three days of her dying, the dealers were brought in to give quotes on the remainder of her possessions.

'You've sold a lifetime of memories,' I had cried in horror over the phone lines.

'Well, they're mine to do with as I like,' had been the swift rejoinder. 'Sure your mother did not even leave a will, so you wasted your time hanging around for her to die.'

That was the last conversation I had with him until social services contacted me to say that he was showing signs of senility and would I visit? It was a phone call he had asked them to make, expecting that my well-ingrained habit of obedience would still be in place.

I did go to his house then, against my better judgement, only to find that his charm had worked on a new generation of women. Holding court to a trio of females – his young pretty social worker, his daily carer and one elderly friend – he smiled at me complacently as I walked into the sitting room.

'Well, if it's not my wee daughter come to visit her old dad,' he exclaimed with a note of triumph in his voice that only I could hear. There was no trace of gratitude in his mocking tones.

Sitting now in his house, I felt his presence begin to leave as the air blown in through the windows cleansed the rooms. I realized that there was nothing here for me – nothing to remind me of the past, nothing to comfort me and nothing to make me afraid. Not one of my mother's possessions was left except for her desk, in which were the notebook, those letters and the three photographs.

I searched the sitting room in vain for more pictures of my mother and of me, something that linked me to my past but there were none. Instead on the coffee table I came across photographs from a more recent time. They showed my father with a group of friends in the sitting room of his new house, obviously celebrating. There were bottles of beer on the table, smiles on the faces of the revellers and glasses held in their hands. On the dining table in the photograph, I could see an assortment of cards on display. Was it his birthday, I wondered. Then, picking up my father's magnifying glass, I peered at the tiny print. No, they were 'Welcome to your New Home' cards. A housewarming party had been held six weeks after my mother's death.

I looked at the photographs and the letter again. Slowly I tore the letter up, hoping its destruction would erase its words from my head. Even as I did so I knew it was a useless act; the words it contained were already imprinted on my memory and the contents would continue to haunt me long after I had left my father's house.

I could not bring myself to destroy the photographs and found myself staring at the one taken when I was a baby again. I was too young when it had been taken to remember the day my mother and I had posed for it. It was a professional photo-graph, taken when Antoinette was around a year old. She was sitting on her mother's knee while Ruth, aged thirty years, dressed in a square-necked dress with her shoulder-length hair falling in loose waves, held her with both hands. Ruth's head was slightly bent but the slight smile on her face could be clearly seen as she looked down at her baby with an obvious pride. There was an unmistakable glow of happiness surrounding the baby and the woman that radiated, nearly half a century later, from the faded print.

The chubby little girl dressed in a pretty silk dress, a tuft of fine hair on her head and a wide toothless grin stretched across her face, sat contently with one pudgy hand grasping a rattle. She looked like the child she was then, a much loved small person, and she beamed radiantly in the direction of the camera.

I thought briefly how neither my mother nor the baby she held could have foreseen how their lives would change and with a sigh, turned the picture face down and placed it on the table.

I thought of the shadow cast over that baby's life and the childhood she had endured. I thought of her decline when, as a teenager, she was no longer able to cope with the rejection she received over and over again from her mother and how she had gradually slid into a black place.

I saw again the image of that bleak bedsitter where Antoinette, huddled in bed, had lost the ability to wake and face a new day. I felt the terror that had finally imprisoned her, the terror of a world that had become inhabited with her enemies.

Chapter Twenty-Two

An hour after the doctor visited her in her bedsitter and slid the needle into her arm, Antoinette entered hospital for the second time. She was again admitted to the psychiatric wing of the forbidding mental hospital that stood in gloomy splendour on the outskirts of Belfast.

The psychiatric ward stood apart from the main building of the hospital and had a light airy décor that gave the patients there the illusion that it was a different world to the one the inmates of the long-stay wards inhabited. But the threat of the main building, the huge red-brick monument of a bygone age, always hung over them, for they knew that should they not respond to treatment it would only take a few minutes for them to be transferred to that other world; a world of barred windows, shabby uniforms and of mind-numbing drugs.

Antoinette was admitted to a side ward of the psychiatric wing. The following day she had her first electric shock treatment.

Her head hurt, nausea rose in her throat and she vomited into a small bowl that was held nearby. She opened her eyes briefly and saw a hazy figure in a blue and white dress. She could hear a jumble of meaningless sounds and a word that kept being repeated – 'Antoinette' – but she no longer recognized it as her name.

Gradually some physical strength returned but with it came the whispering voices. They were in the room, terrifying her. Desperate to escape them, she threw herself from the bed and fled from the ward and down the corridor. The whispers followed her. Her long hospital nightgown flapped around her bare ankles, almost tripping her as she tried to outrun her pursuers. She only stopped when, blinded by her fear, she slammed into a wall. She slid down it with her fists clenched tightly over her ears as she tried uselessly to block out the sounds inside her head.

Hands reached out to lift her. She heard that name again and crouched on the floor with both arms raised to protect herself from her tormentors. She wanted to beg them not to hurt her, but she had lost the ability to form words. Instead an animal keening, chilling in its desperation, left her mouth.

Another needle pricked her arm. Then she was picked up and placed into a wheelchair, almost unconscious. She was taken back to her room where, mercifully, she slept.

When she woke a man was sitting beside her bed.

'Ah, so you're awake, are you?' he said, as her eyes flickered open. Confused she tried to focus on him but his words made very little sense to her.

'Don't you remember me, Antoinette? I was one of the doctors who treated you when you were here two years ago.'

She didn't remember. She did not know where she had been two years ago or where she was now, and she turned her head away to block out the sound of the words. His was just another voice that lied to her and mocked her. She heard the murmur of it and, with her face still averted, squeezed her eyes tightly shut in that hope that he would simply disappear. In the end, she felt him leave. Then she opened her eyes again and looked fearfully at her surroundings.

The curtains were drawn back from her bed and she saw people passing by and felt them staring at her. She pulled herself angrily out of bed, shuffled to the curtains and pulled them shut. This was her space; she wanted no intruders in it.

Later the nurses helped her put on a dressing gown, then held her gently by the arms and led her to the canteen. Once there, she turned her chair to face the wall. If she couldn't see other people, she reasoned, they could not see her.

Her mind was jumbled. She was dazed and disorientated but she still searched for the white light of oblivion. She wanted to crawl into it but the treatment had made her forget why.

The nurses tried to talk to her but she refused to speak in the hope that if she didn't, then she also would also cease to hear the voices around her. When food was held out to her she shook her head vehemently but only a whimper escaped her throat. Tablets were placed in her mouth and a glass of water held for her to sip. She swallowed them and then retreated into sleep.

It was time for her next electric shock treatment. She had no idea how long it had been since the last one, or how long she had been in the ward at all. The nurses said it would help her but Antoinette no longer cared. She had abandoned the real world and had no desire to return to it. Her days were spent in a drug-induced daze and at night she was helped to sleep by more and stronger pills. Still she refused to talk.

Nurses would sit by her bedside, hold her hand, repeat her name but the only response they got was another bout of silent weeping, as tears fell down her face.

'Antoinette, talk to me,' the female psychiatrist pleaded for the third time that morning. 'We want to help you, we want you to get well again. Won't you help us? Don't you want to get better?'

Antoinette finally turned her head and looked into the face of her doctor for the first time. She had heard her voice before. The nurses had brought her to this psychiatrist several times in the hope that some bond would be forged and the therapy could start.

For the first time in three weeks, she spoke in a croaky but childish voice. 'You can't help me.'

'Why not?'

There was a long pause before Antoinette finally replied. 'I have a secret, a secret. Only I know what it is. You don't know.'

'What is the secret?'

'We are all dead. I'm dead, and so are you. We've died.'

'If we are all dead, then where are we now?'

'We are in hell, but nobody knows – only me.' Her eyes met those of her psychiatrist but she didn't see her. Instead she saw only her ghosts. She starting rocking backwards and forwards, her hands grasping her knees. Her voice rose in a chant, 'We're dead. We are all dead.' Over and over she sang it, until it made her laugh because she knew that the doctor did not believe her.

The doctor asked in a calm, soft voice, 'Why do you think you are the only person who thinks that?'

But Antoinette had withdrawn deep into herself again and turned her face away. The doctor called for the nurses to take her back to the ward and her therapy was over.

Back on the ward she drew the curtains round her bed and sat in the middle of it. Clasping her hands over her knees, she rocked back and forward again while high-pitched giggles escaped her as she thought about her secret and how she was the only person who knew it to be true.

The next day they increased her sedatives and continued the electric shock treatment.

There was no sign of her depression lifting. Instead, the four sessions of an electric current being run through her brain had only made her retreat deeper into herself. If its purpose was to cloud her memory and help her to forget the past until she was able to deal with it gradually, it had failed. For now, the nightmares that haunted her sleep penetrated her waking hours.

The horrific sensation of being out of control, of being chased and of falling now overcame her during the day, increasing her panic and the whispers that taunted her were never silent. She hid in her bed with the curtains drawn, trying to find a refuge from her terrors, and refused to speak, thinking if she was never heard she would become invisible.

When she was taken from her bed to the canteen, she faced the wall in the belief that her wish had been granted and she was now invisible. And she did not want to see all the people around her who were dead but didn't know it.

* * *

The fifth electric shock seemed to bring a result. This time she did not try to run as soon as consciousness returned, the clouds in her head lifted and she knew one thing: she was thirsty.

'Nurse, can I have a drink of tea?' she asked.

The ward sister was so surprised at the request that she hurried to the kitchen and made it herself. She held out the cup to Antoinette.

Taking it in both hands, she sipped tentatively. She struggled to see through the fog in her brain, trying to understand where she was and who she was.

'Is there anything else you want, Antoinette?' asked the ward sister.

'My mother,' she answered. 'I want my mother.'

A silence hung for a second in the air.

'She can't come quite yet,' said the sister in a comforting voice. 'But I'm sure she will soon, especially when she hears how well you're doing. You must be getting better – this is the first time you've spoken to me since you arrived.'

'Yes,' said Antoinette without emotion, and sipped again at her drink.

Chapter Twenty-Three

'Wake up.'

Antoinette felt a slight shake of her shoulder. Her eyes flickered open and she found herself looking into blue eyes set under sandy brows. It was a familiar face – but who was it?

'It's me, Gus. Don't you remember me?'

As she heard the voice again, she recognized Gus, the girl she had made friends with on the first occasion she had stayed in the hospital two years before. She looked at her groggily and saw the open friendliness on her face. Antoinette stretched out a hesitant hand to her. She felt the warm flesh of the other girl's hand and knew she was real.

'Gus,' she said, confused. Gus couldn't be here. She had left a long time ago. Antoinette could remember her parents coming to collect her.

Gus saw the puzzled look on her face and gave her hand a light squeeze. 'I'm back,' she said, answering her friend's unspoken question.

'Why?'

Gus rolled up her sleeve and showed the thin scars that rose in jagged lines from the wrist to several inches above the elbow. Antoinette could see that old ones had been opened up again; many were barely healed.

'Why?' she repeated.

Tears brimmed in Gus's eyes and she hastily brushed them aside. Antoinette raised her other hand and gently stroked the face looking down at her, wiping away a tear drop as she did so.

'I'm back for the third time. You know we all come back,' Gus said simply. 'You know, sometimes I feel I can't get any lower. When I've hit the bottom, I try and tell myself that the only way forward is to start climbing up. On other days, just as I think I've clawed myself out of the black hole and I'm standing on the edge, I feel myself falling back in.'

Antoinette thought of her own nightmare where invisible claws tried to drag her down and understood exactly what her friend meant. She understood where she had been. What she did not understand was what had driven Gus to such desperate measures. 'But why, Gus? You have lovely parents, a family that care for you. Why you?' She struggled to understand.

'Why am I screaming silently? Why do I do this to myself when I have everything you would die to have, is that what you are asking? If I knew, if I only knew, I could stop. But it's the only time I feel in control. My parents do everything they can to understand, everything they can to help, but the only time I feel in charge of my own life is when I cut myself.' A look of deep sadness mixed with total bewilderment crossed her face. 'So what happened to you?' She turned Antoinette's hand over and looked at the wrists but saw no fresh scars there.

There was a long pause before Antoinette replied at last, 'My mother took him back.'

Gus knew who *he* was. She squeezed her friend's hand. 'Then what happened?'

'I don't know. Everything just got muddled and the next thing I knew I woke up in here. I get so tired – tired of trying to make sense of my life and tired of trying to survive.' And, as though to prove the point, she felt her eyes begin to close but this time as she drifted off to sleep she felt more peaceful than she had done for months. Gus, she felt, understood in a way that the doctors never could, for she also lived in the same black place.

The nurses saw the two girls talking and left them alone. If Gus was breaking through their youngest patient's defences, they did not want to interfere. They knew that patients could often have a better understanding of each other than anyone else, and that the friendships that sprung up in hospital could help in the healing process.

It did not take Gus very long to piece together what had been the final reason for Antoinette's breakdown. When Antoinette had woken from her sleep, Gus returned, sat on her friend's bed and looked sternly at her.

'Look, I'm sick, but you are just unhappy. Your misery has been too much to bear so you've tried to disappear inside yourself.' Gus spoke as though she was determined to break down all the barriers that Antoinette had erected around herself. 'What you have to understand is that people often are unkind to those they have wronged. People don't like having a guilty conscience and they resent their victim for giving it to them. That's your mother, all right. It seems to me that your father is different.' Gus grimaced with dislike at the thought of a man she had never met and continued, 'He just despises you for letting him do what he did to you. When you were little you had no choice. But you do now.' She paused to make sure that Antoinette was paying attention and then said gravely, 'You have to get away from them or at least put a stop to how they treat you. It's possible that if you had stood up to him, shown him he had no effect on you, then he would have left you alone. And as for your mother ... well, she would always have followed him and she'll never change.'

'What makes you think that my father despises me?' asked Antoinette, stung.

'Because of what I feel about my parents. They would do anything to make me better. They love me whatever I do to hurt them. They buy me anything I want. They blame themselves for what is wrong with me. Although I love them, I can't help feeling contemptuous of them for it.'

'I'm scared, Gus,' Antoinette admitted. 'Scared of being out there.'

'How can it be any worse than what you live with now? Don't you see what your parents do to you? They undermine you at every opportunity. They bully you and reduce you to something pitiful. But there's a life out there, so take it up with both hands or you will end up back in this hospital over and over again. Now come on, it's time for dinner.'

Gus smiled and helped Antoinette up and to get dressed. They went together to the dining room and, for the first time since she had been admitted, Antoinette ate without looking at the wall.

Chapter Twenty-Four

As Gus and Antoinette were sitting together in the residents' lounge, a nurse approached them. 'Girls, there's a dance being arranged for the patients in the main building tomorrow night. Patients from this ward are allowed to go over and join in. Do you want to go?'

Antoinette started to shake her head. It didn't sound very enjoyable to her. The patients in the main building were permanent residents, those with such severe problems that they would probably never venture into the outside world again.

'Oh, come on,' said Gus, coaxing her. 'It'll be fun. We can get dressed up and enjoy ourselves for a change.'

'I don't know,' Antoinette replied doubtfully. 'What will I wear?' She thought of her meagre wardrobe. The waistbands of her skirts and trousers now dug into her while her jumpers clung too tightly. The stodgy hospital food had increased her weight by over ten pounds and she was conscious that her figure was much fuller. Her clinging clothes might have brought admiring glances from some of the male patients but that only made her feel uncomfortable. She was also aware that the ward sister flashed the odd disapproving look whenever she had made an effort to look nice.

'I'll lend you a blouse,' said Gus. 'Lots of my things will fit you. We can dress up and get ready together. Make an evening of it.'

Suddenly Antoinette felt a flicker of something approaching excitement. It was a long time since she had experienced fun far less sought it out.

The following day both girls forgot their problems as they enjoyed getting ready for a night out like any normal teenagers. Gus chose a long-sleeved blouse which covered the marks of the self-mutilation and lent her friend a charcoal grey skirt and a scarlet blouse. When they were dressed, they carefully inspected their faces in the mirror above the wash-basin and made themselves look as glamorous as possible. With her hair backcombed and lacquered, Antoinette felt young and pretty for the first time in many weeks. The two girls inspected each other, checking that shoes were polished and stockings unladdered, and when they had pronounced each other ready, they made their way to the lounge.

The other patients were already there and were gathered in small groups. A buzz of animated chatter livened up the lounge. Everyone was dressed in what finery they had managed to put together and there was an unaccustomed air of gaiety and excitement.

Two uniformed nurses, who also seemed relaxed and happy with the break in their routine, led them to the main building. The old part of the hospital smelt different to the psychiatric ward: it had the nasty aroma of unwashed bodies and cheap disinfectant, and the bitter tang of medication seemed to be everywhere. But Antoinette did not wrinkle her nose at it; she was caught up in the cheerfulness of the other patients and had even gone as far as promising a dance to one of the male inmates.

Two doors led into the huge room where the dance was to be held but it quickly became apparent to everyone's consternation that the men and women were to be separated. The men had to join a queue at one side and the woman another, and then enter through different doors.

'What's going on?' whispered Antoinette to Gus, nervous.

'They must be bringing up the other patients. The ones from the long-stay wards here in the main building,' Gus whispered back.

'How will we all stay together if we're separated?' Suddenly the men from the psychiatric ward looked safe and familiar.

'Join your line, please!' called a nurse. Gus and Antoinette went with the other women to stand by their door. The sound of footsteps and chatter heralded the arrival of the women from the long-stay wards. Immediately the girls felt embarrassed that they had dressed up as the inmates arrived and joined the queue behind them. These women wore shapeless uniforms, the only clothes allowed for long-term patients, but they seemed unaware of their shabby dresses, thick stockings and flat scuffed shoes as they talked excitedly to each other. Some were quiet, their heads downcast, lost in the dreams that sedatives give as they shuffled silently along to join the queue. One pressed in close to Antoinette and she smelt the sweet cloying smell of the liquid drug Paraldehyde on the other woman's breath. She quickly turned her head away, nauseated.

Before she had time to think about the fates of these women, the doors swung open and the crowd surged forward, pushing Antoinette and Gus with the rest of their group through the doors.

The other psychiatric patients looked at each other appalled – they had thought that their ward would be an elite little group that danced and mixed with each other while ignoring the others. They hadn't wanted to fraternize with the long-stayers.

Gus and Antoinette saw the anxiety on the older women's faces and hung on to each other, trying not to giggle. They had the confidence of youth that as soon as the music started, the men from their ward would make a beeline for them and they would be the belles of the ball.

They were wrong. While the men from the psychiatric ward had the advantage that most of them had learnt to dance at school, they did not possess the speed of the men from the main building. It seemed that no matter how sedated they were or what mental problems had led them to a life inside the hospital, the sight of so many women dressed up prettily lent them wings.

The opening notes of the first record acted as a starting pistol. Ignoring the women wearing uniforms, the male patients from the long-term wards converged as one on Antoinette's group.

Antoinette quailed as the men rushed forward. A tall patient with flushed cheeks reached her first, sprinting towards her on his long legs, clumsy as a newborn colt. Without stopping to talk, he grabbed her arm and whirled her into a dance, one that only he knew the steps to.

He's obviously confused dancing with the three-legged race, she thought, too surprised to resist. Not that she could have stopped him. With huge enthusiasm, her partner held her firmly and ran at full speed to the end of the hall where only the wall saved her from falling. Then, with more strength than skill, he turned her round and repeated the exercise, running her back down the room at full pelt.

At last, the music stopped and the wild dash up and down the room came to an end. Her partner released her reluctantly.

The wide grin on his face seemed to indicate that this was the best time he had ever had and Antoinette could not help herself smiling back at a man who appeared so happy.

She glanced back at the patients from the ward, and saw that some of the men were doubled up with merriment at her predicament. She glared at them and then looked beseechingly at the others. As the second record started up, the men from her ward took a leaf out of the book of the long-stayers and this time moved faster. Antoinette sighed with relief when Danny, her favourite male nurse, grasped her arm before her previous partner could make another claim.

The next dance was a jive, something she was good at and, as Danny swung her in time to a fast beat, she felt the music move her and her inhibitions leave. Round and round she spun, under his arm, round his back and into his arms again. To her delight, loud applause broke out as the dance came to an end.

'Stay with him,' said one of the other nurses. 'It's good entertainment.'

Antoinette readily agreed. She gave her partner from the first dance a cheerful wave as she jived near him and grinned when he returned it. It was a pleasure to see the long-term inmates enjoying themselves. As the evening progressed, discipline slackened and the patients of her ward were allowed to stay together.

Gus and Antoinette suddenly noticed a group of woman who were watching the dancing but had not joined in. Then she saw that on the opposite side of the room there were some men, dressed in equally shapeless uniforms as the woman, standing nervously together. It seemed that without any firm direction from the staff, they had no idea what to do and simply stood on the sidelines, bewildered.

'We can't have that, can we?' said Gus with a grin. 'My mother always told me that the point of a good party is that everyone has fun.'

Antoinette went up to Danny and pointed out the wallflowers. 'We want them to enjoy themselves as well,' she said. 'The dance is for everyone.'

'What do you want me to do about it?' he asked.

The girls' brows furrowed with concentration, and then Gus came up with an idea.

'The congo, of course! You don't have to know any dance steps for that. You're staff, Danny. You start it off and we'll pull everyone in.' She turned to the rest of the patients from the ward. 'Come on, everyone. There's nothing special about us. Let's mingle and make sure we all enjoy ourselves.'

The music started. Danny took charge and Antoinette followed behind, clasping his waist. As they started sashaying round the room, Antoinette grabbed her first partner by the hand and showed him how to join the line. Gus pulled one of the quiet women from the sidelines on board and then everyone joined in. Soon, over fifty people were swaying to the congo in a long line that swerved and wriggled in time to the music. Round and round they went and then, to cries of 'one more time!', they did it twice more. Suddenly there were smiles and laughter that broke through the daze of Paraldehyde and barbiturates and the patients from the main building seemed to come to life. There were loud whoops of glee as they whirled and danced.

For the grand finale, there was the hokey-cokey instead of the last waltz. It wasn't easy for so many people to form a circle and when they did, right feet swung out and left feet swung in a rhythm that had little in common with the music. Nobody cared.

'Hey, Danny!' yelled a patient whose wide cheeky grin showed his total enjoyment. 'Good thing the people on the outside can't see how we party on the inside. They'd all want to come in if they did!'

Chapter Twenty-Five

Two nights after the dance, the night sister woke Antoinette up.

'Antoinette,' she whispered, 'it's your friend Gus. We've had to send for her parents. Will you sit with her until they come?'

Antoinette blinked groggily and looked up at the nurse in confusion. She knew that it was not time to get up; the ward was still almost in darkness.

'Come with me. I'll explain in the kitchen.'

Antoinette slipped her arms into the dressing gown the nurse held out, shuffled feet into her slippers and followed the night sister. She could guess that something serious had happened but what, she didn't know.

But they told me to sit with Gus, she reassured herself. So if she had done something really terrible – she shied away from the word suicide – they wouldn't have woken me in the middle of the night.

'Is she … all right?' she asked timidly.

The sister glanced at her and read the concern on her face. 'Don't worry, your friend will live. We found her in time.'

She told Antoinette that Gus had climbed into a bath filled with hot water and then, with a razor she had stolen from a locker belonging to one of the male patients, had proceeded to slash both her arms. Thinking she would be undisturbed, she had cut and slashed in a frenzy of self-mutilation. There were so many cuts that the water had turned scarlet.

'She's a very sick girl,' said the sister sadly. 'There's nothing more we can do for her in this ward. Both her parents are coming for her but it will take some time for them to get here. I don't want her left alone but there's only one other nurse on duty. And Gus keeps asking for you.'

Antoinette couldn't hide how upset the news made her. The sister looked at sympathetically.

'Will you do it?' she asked.

'Of course I will,' Antoinette said quickly. 'Gus has helped me so much since I've been here. But I don't understand why her parents are being sent for.' She knew that suicide attempts usually meant a transfer to the main building and the twilight, drug-heavy existence of the patients she had seen at the dance.

'Didn't she tell you? Her mother is a psychiatrist. We think she may be the best person to help her now. Gus has everything she could wish for except – ' the sister paused '– happiness.'

Antoinette crept quietly into the side ward where Gus had been placed. Her friend lay tucked under the bedclothes, her red hair contrasting with the pallor of her face. Her arms were bandaged and lay stiffly outside the sheets. Antoinette sat down next to her, took the hand nearest her and stroked it lightly.

'Gus, it's me. Can you hear me?' she asked, stricken to see her friend in this state. Gus had seemed so upbeat lately – she had really enjoyed herself on the night of the dance. The sandy head turned slowly and two blue eyes looked directly into hers. Antoinette saw the despair that was written into them. She felt answering tears come to her own eyes but blinked them away. Crying was not going to help her friend.

'My parents are coming,' said Gus quietly, through dry lips.

'Yes, I know.'

'They'll send me away to a nice private place. Right now, they'll be busy on the phone making sure they do the right thing.'

'You never told me that your mother's a psychiatrist.' It was all Antoinette could think of to say.

'Didn't I? Well, it's not the most important thing to me. It's the most important thing to my mother, though. She places great importance on her work and her patients' needs.' She sighed. 'She doesn't see me. She sees I need help but she doesn't see me. I've made my mother a failure in her eyes. What kind of doctor is she if she can't help her own daughter? What she should ask herself is why she failed as a mother.' Gus looked at her and smiled weakly. 'This must all seem ridiculous to you. I know she's nothing like the one you have – but I'm not as strong as you.'

Startled that anyone should think she was strong, Antoinette thought Gus must be joking but realized that her friend was unlikely to capable of humour at such a moment. 'I'm not strong,' she retorted.

'Yes, you are. You're still alive, aren't you?' The sandy head turned away.

Antoinette knew her friend had finished talking. She sat silently holding Gus's hand until the nurse came.

'Gus, your parents are here,' said the sister. 'They have come to take you home.'

'Not for long,' Gus retorted. 'Mummy has her patients to look after, ones with real problems. You know, nurse, it's a nice private clinic for me. My mother can pay for the experts to look after me while she earns her money looking after people who need her.'

The nurse had no answer to give but just started to put out clothes for Gus to wear.

Antoinette knew it was time for her to leave but she wanted to stay with her friend and walk with her to the entrance.

The nurse, who understood how close the girls had become, said kindly, 'Antoinette, you stay here and then you can walk to the door with us and say goodbye to your friend there.' Seeing the unhappiness on her youngest patient's face, she sighed. 'When Gus has gone, we'll go to the kitchen and I'll make us both a nice milky drink of hot chocolate.'

A hot drink was no compensation for what was happening to Gus, but Antoinette appreciated the kindly gesture and gave her a wobbly smile. A few minutes later, the nurse led the two girls to the lobby where an elegant woman dressed in dark trousers and matching jumper was waiting.

That must be Gus's mother, thought Antoinette. She looks like someone who never dresses in a hurry. She looks like someone who always wants to make the right impression.

It was time to part. Gus turned to her and squeezed her hand. 'Goodbye and get better. Remember what I told you. You're stronger than you think.'

Then, with a quick hug, the two girls parted. Gus walked over to the woman and the two of them went quietly out of the hospital. The last sight Antoinette had of Gus was a flash of red hair as the black sedan that had collected her drove slowly away.

* * *

One week later Antoinette's dream returned.

She moaned in her sleep at the menace in her nightmare. As she began to fall and the mocking voices in her dream rose to a crescendo. Her control slipped. She came to semi-consciousness and stumbled half-asleep out of bed, desperate to escape the demons which had invaded her mind once more. But there was no evading them and their voices grew louder as she lurched down the corridor to the lounge. She threw herself into a chair and put her hands over her ears to shut them out, drawing up her legs under her chin.

The nurse found her rocking back and forwards moaning with despair, and saw that her brief spell of normality had come to an end.

The doctors resumed electric shock treatments. This time she did not run, but neither did she talk.

Chapter Twenty-Six

Tim tapped his feet and spun the heavy swivel chair round and round to the sound of the music in his head.

Antoinette's gaze never left him as she followed his movements. As the chair rotated again and again, she stared at him. When the chair's back hid her view of his face and only a glimpse of a thin shoulder could be seen, she waited for the chair to complete its turn so that she could see him again.

Behind his wire-framed glasses, his eyes glinted.

He sees into my head, thought Antoinette. He can trespass into my thoughts. She covered her eyes with her hands. If I can't see him, he can't see me, she thought desperately. But almost at once, she stopped believing it and she couldn't stop herself saying, 'Stop. Stop what you're doing.'

They were the first words she had spoken for over a week and they were strangely expressionless. The total lack of feeling in them carried a warning and the patients' sitting room became silent.

Antoinette felt her body become rigid with concentration as she stared unwaveringly at the boy in the swivel chair. She was vaguely aware that the male nurse in the room half stood up as if sensing trouble but her gaze remained fixed on Tim. Lost in his own world and at the mercy of his own memories, he spun the chair once more. For a split second their eyes met. Tim giggled.

And she heard its mocking sound coming from a thousand throats and it seemed to vibrate all about the jumble inside her head. Unable to stop herself, she screamed and then a snarl of rage tore out of her throat. Her only desire at that moment was to tip him from the chair, bring its metal base down on his head and stop the derisive laughter for ever.

She darted forward and grabbed the chair so that the boy was thrown to the ground and, with a strength fired by her enormous rage, she began to lift it. She knew that she would pick it up and then dash it down on top of him – but before she could do anything else, the male nurse moved and grasped her by the arm.

'Let it go,' he commanded. 'Put it down now.'

Her strength was no match for his, and he prized her fingers from it easily. She felt herself shake as though every muscle in her body trembled. The nurse guided her carefully into the chair.

The rage which had lain dormant for so many years had finally surfaced and the force with which it had burst out of her started clearing the fog from her mind. As they receded, she saw a skinny form lying on the floor. Tim lay where she had thrown him, lost so deeply in his own world that her fury had not even penetrated it.

The lounge was in an uproar. Antoinette sat bewildered, hardly remembering what she had done.

The male staff nurse put his hand on her shoulder, then looked for a female patient he could safely entrust her with so that she could be kept calm until the ward sister came on duty.

'Dianne,' he said, 'could you take Antoinette for coffee and sit with her?'

Dianne was a woman in her mid-thirties who had improved steadily since she had entered the hospital and the nurse obviously thought that her motherly aura would keep Antoinette steady.

Dianne did as she was told, took the shaken girl by the hand and led her to the canteen. She sat Antoinette in a chair, made two coffees, then returned quickly to the table.

'Come on, drink that up,' she said kindly. Then seeing that the teenager still seemed to be locked in a world of her own, she lit two cigarettes and passed one across the table. 'Have one of these.'

Antoinette did not smoke but she took it gratefully. If nothing else, it gave her something to do with her hands.

Diane looked at her sympathetically. 'I think you'll start to get better now, if you want my opinion. All that anger that you must have had inside had to come out, you know.'

Antoinette remained silent, her body still shaking as tremors ran through her. Gradually the mist that had clouded her mind for so many weeks was beginning to recede. She looked blankly at the older woman without recognition.

'We've talked before,' said Dianne, noticing her bewilderment. 'You don't remember me, do you?'

Antoinette shook her head, feeling even more confused. She wanted to remember, for there was something about the older woman she felt she could trust. Something about the face and its sympathetic expression radiated more warmth and understanding than she had ever seen in her mother's. She knew that Dianne was the kind of woman her mother would scorn as common – her accent showed she came from a rough part of town – but Antoinette already knew that her own values were different from her mother's. She had learnt that it is who you are, not where you come from, that counts.

Dianne took a drag on her cigarette. The deep lines etched on her face and the badly styled hair streaked with grey made her look older than her years. Antoinette suddenly realized that her companion was wearing the uniform of a different ward, a fact that momentarily disconcerted her.

Seeing the puzzled expression on the girl's face, Dianne said gently, 'I'm in Ward F1 and I was there when you were a patient there nearly three years ago. I can tell you don't remember. You were such a lonely confused girl then, I felt so sorry for you. But when you left, I hoped you would stay away. What happened?'

Antoinette struggled to remember the woman sitting opposite her. She had met people from that ward before. It housed the milder cases of sectioned patients, some of whom were placed there instead of serving a short prison sentence. Certainly it was not home to anyone dangerous and when patients were considered to be on the road to recovery, they were often allowed to visit the psychiatric ward with its coffee lounge and generally relaxed air.

'We talked the last time you were in,' said Dianne. 'Danny was worried when they released you – he thought it was too early. Tell me what brought you back here.'

Not remembering any conversations between Dianne and herself, Antoinette had no idea what the older woman knew.

Ignoring Antoinette's silence, Dianne continued as though there were two people taking part in the conversation instead of just one. 'You told me about your father, how he had gone to prison for what he did to you, then you left here to live with your mother.'

'And my mother told me I had to leave.'

Dianne didn't need to be told more and gently touched her on the hand. 'You'll get better, you'll get over them. You must.

Don't let them win.' She drew on her cigarette and looked at the younger girl reflectively. 'You might not believe me now but one day you will be happy.'

She's right, Antoinette thought grimly. I don't believe her. Happiness was not something she could imagine ever feeling again. She tried to think of something to say. She had no desire to talk about her parents but she knew Dianne was not going to allow her to slip away into silence. Hoping to shift the conversation away from herself, she said at last, 'Why are you here?'

'I killed my husband. You'd read about it in the newspapers when you were here before. Remember? I stabbed the bastard to death.'

'Why?' asked Antoinette, with the first glimmer of interest.

'Usual story. He beat me when he was drunk and he was always drunk. I would look in the mirror and see a woman I no longer recognized – one with a black eye, a split lip, or both – then I would be stupid enough to wonder what I'd done wrong. You know, love, you might not believe it now but when I met him I was a pretty girl. I had plenty of boyfriends then but I had to choose a no-good bastard like him.'

'Why did you stay?' Antoinette knew her mother never would have. She would have left her husband if he had ever laid a finger on her, she thought bitterly. It was only me she didn't mind him hitting.

'Because every time he hit me, the next day he was so apologetic, he would beg me not to leave him and then the next few months were honeymoon time again. I fell in love, if that is what you want to call it, eight times in as many years and every other year got a child from it. But then, when the kids were older he went for them with a belt. No one goes for my kids. So I left him and we went to stay with my dad.' Dianne saw she now had Antoinette's complete attention and continued with her story. 'Well, he came round, didn't he? Drunk, he was that night. Pushed right past my dad and knocked my little one over. I picked up the bread knife and stuck it in him. And you know the worst thing? I enjoyed it. That red mist came down, I saw the fear on his face when I went for him and I felt great. It was only when the police came that I felt sorry.' She paused and then added, 'But not sorry for doing it. Sorry that my kids had to be taken into care.'

'Why did they put you in here?' Antoinette knew that in her previous life she had read somewhere of a case where the woman had killed an abusive husband. The barrister had pleaded a case of self-defence and she had been acquitted.

'Because once I started, I couldn't stop. I enjoyed it that much. They said I'd put wounds in him after he was dead. But he had gone for my kids and no one was going to harm them.' She suddenly realized who she was confiding in and placed her hand over Antoinette's. 'Sorry, love. Everyone's different.'

But Antoinette didn't even understand what she meant.

Chapter Twenty-Seven

In 1961, paranoia was seen as dangerous. Antoinette had attacked Tim with no provocation but no account was taken of the fact that she had been given an electric shock treatment that morning and neither was any notice given to the opinion of the psychiatrists who had already questioned the suitability of that particular treatment for her. It only took a few phone calls from the ward sister – a woman of the old school who had little time for the freedom given to patients on the new psychiatric wing – for a transfer to be arranged.

Antoinette watched while a nurse packed her few belongings. 'Where am I going?' she asked.

The nurse did not reply but kept her head bent as she finished her task.

Frightened, Antoinette repeated the question. 'Where am I going?'

'Somewhere where they can look after you better.'

The icy clipped tones came from behind her. Antoinette spun round to see who had spoken. The ward sister was standing a few feet away, watching her. A woman in her early thirties whose thin hair was worn scraped back in a tight knot, she held her body so stiffly that she seemed to be encased in steel under her blue uniform. From the day she had arrived,

Antoinette had always thought there was a cold antipathy from the ward sister that was more than simple dislike. Every member of staff was privy to a patient's case history and she had felt instinctively that the ward sister had very little sympathy for hers. She had felt her eyes follow her when she walked about and had seen a smirk cross her face when Antoinette talked to male nurses or patients. Somehow Antoinette had always felt that the sister was looking for her to make a mistake, something she could pounce on. Now she finally had the excuse she needed and Antoinette saw the flash of satisfaction in her eyes as they met hers. But it was the other who looked away first.

Antoinette was to be moved early that evening, at a time when the other patients were busy with their visitors. The sight of a patient that they had known being transferred to the long-stay section of the hospital was upsetting for everyone, including the staff.

Once her locker was emptied, she sat on her bed with the curtains drawn. Her tea was served by nurses who hastily placed a tray by her side and then left as quickly as possible. Each time one appeared, Antoinette asked the same question.

'Where am I going? Where are you sending me?'

But nobody wanted to tell her.

The other patients avoided her; they knew without being told that Antoinette was being sent to the place they feared most. Everyone knew that those who didn't recover would share her fate – a transfer to the main building.

When the evening drew in they came for her.

The ward sister and two male orderlies stood by her bed and one of the men picked up her case. Their grim faces told her that patients who kicked and screamed and protested against their transfer would be quickly subdued. Antoinette had no intention of giving the ward sister the satisfaction of crying but she still summoned up the strength to ask her question again.

'Where am I going?'

This time, she did not bother to avoid her gaze. Instead she said, with a smile that almost looked triumphant, 'You are going to be transferred to ward F3A.'

Antoinette felt her body go icy cold. Ward F3 was where the hospital put long-term patients whom everyone believed had no hope of recovering. It was the ward where women were shut away and forgotten. They wouldn't leave until they grew old and feeble or died. Everyone knew where in the main hospital that ward was. It was hidden from curious eyes behind doors that were firmly shut but the barred windows could be clearly seen from the grounds. Although no patient in Antoinette's unit had ever caught a glimpse of the inside, they had all heard stories of how it was in there.

In those dark rooms, it was said, as many as thirty women were left in the care of only two nurses. Locked into specially designed wooden chairs for hours at a time, they would sit staring blankly into space. It was in there that drugs were given not to heal but to keep the inmates docile, and to ensure their passivity, indiscriminate courses of electric shock were administered. The woman in these wards could never complain. They had no one to complain to. These wards were inhabited by people who had long ago forfeited their rights when they had been abandoned by their families. They were the lost people, forgotten by the outside world.

The inmates of ward F3 were rarely seen. Not for them escorted walks in the spacious grounds or mingling with other patients in the canteen; they were marched three times a day to their own area in the main dining room and when their meal was finished, they were marched back again. Once, when she was in the main building, Antoinette had seen a straggling procession of women from that ward: shapeless uniforms hung slackly on their drooping bodies as two nurses armed with batons escorted them to their section of the dining room. With downcast eyes and in silence, they had shuffled past Antoinette like thirty grey ghosts. The only sound was the flapping of loose slippers.

As well as women who were considered to have no hope of ever being able to leave the hospital and resume a normal life, Ward Female 3A also housed at least two convicted murderesses. They had been judged criminally insane and sentenced to a life in a mental hospital. It was not a fate to be envied. At least in prison, there was hope of remission. But not here.

Antoinette had guessed that her transfer would take her to the main building but this ward was worse than she had ever imagined.

Surely it will only be for a short time, she thought. They just want to punish me. Then I'll be allowed back. 'How long will I be there?' she asked timidly.

'You are being transferred permanently,' was the reply.

Antoinette retreated into silence. It was all she could think of, and she hoped it would protect her. She hid the fear that was beginning to break through her numbness behind an impassive face and waited for the orderly to lead her from the ward.

Outside, the rain fell; it was a gentle spray that Antoinette held her face up to. She felt the damp coolness on her cheeks and thought that if she cried silently, they would think her tears were raindrops. The ambulance which was to transfer her was waiting outside. The orderly helped her in, placed her case beside her, then, refusing to meet her eyes, closed the doors. Antoinette watched the light disappear as they slammed shut on her. Placing her hand on her case for support, she sat upright on the plastic-covered seat.

The engine started and the ambulance rolled along the driveway that took her to the main building.

It was the early part of the year, before the coming of spring brought longer days and warmer nights. The cold penetrated her thin coat but whether it was the damp evening or her fear that made Antoinette shiver, she did not know. All she understood was she was being punished and that finally the words that the voices tormented her with were coming true. In Ward F3A, she would disappear.

Chapter Twenty-Eight

I tried to force myself to put those memories aside but the picture of Antoinette as they took her by the arms and marched her down the long tiled corridor was fixed in my mind. The smell of the hospital odours, disinfectant mingling with cheap soap, stale food and musty air that over the decades had oozed into the very pores of the walls, still lingered in my nostrils. Once the hospital had been a poorhouse for destitute families and when Antoinette had first visited it at the age of fifteen, she had recoiled from the echoes of past misery which still lingered there. The hopelessness of the hundreds of people who had passed through its doors hung like an invisible cloud that wrapped itself around her until she had almost choked on their wretchedness.

I asked myself how I had ever found it inside me to forgive my parents for what had happened to me. I thought of the hours of therapy I had sat through while psychiatrists tried to make me accept the reality of my childhood and the legacy of the abuse my father inflicted on me.

But why did it have to happen, I asked myself. What had made a man become what he had become? At what stage of his childhood had he realized he was different, I wondered. If a child is born unable to walk when do they look at their peers and realize that their contemporaries can run whereas they can only crawl? When does a child born with no sight miss the freedom that seeing gives? At what age does a child who cannot hear know what continuing silence means?

When a sociopath hears his peers talk of feelings he never experiences, does he envy them? Does he wish he could feel the joy from small things that they experience? Or does he feel superior and confuse lack of feelings with strength?

Looking back through the years, I remembered my father's craving to be liked and admired but also his rage when he imagined he had been slighted or snubbed, and I thought that it was the latter.

As an adult I had come to understood who my father really was: a man who imitated feelings to such an extent he believed he had them. He did not grieve for my mother when she died, because he could not understand what he had lost from his life. He was incapable of it. All he knew was that she had become the past, and he only lived in the present and planned for the future. In a way, I pitied him for his inability to feel.

My grandmother had tried to excuse my father's legendary rages on an accident in his childhood – maybe every parent who spawns a monster does – and my mother had often told me the same story, as though it would make me sorry for him and all his acts of cruelty could be excused. When I was older, she expanded on the story, telling me that it was not only his childhood trauma but also the time he had spent serving in the army during the war that had damaged him to the extent that he was not responsible for his actions

Joe was the eldest child in his family, born into the slums of Coleraine. He was a handsome child with a ready smile and an infectious laugh. Tall for his age, with a mop of dark auburn curls, he was the apple of my grandmother's eye. For the first two years at school, his bright enquiring mind had made him popular with his teachers. His reports were good and his mother, who by now had produced two more children, was proud of her eldest. But tragedy struck when he was eight.

My grandmother was lying in bed, heavily pregnant with her fourth child, when she heard a scream followed by a thump. Hurrying into the adjoining room where all three children slept in the double bed, she saw two sleeping bodies not three. Joe had crawled over the bodies of his siblings to the landing where he had tripped and fallen headfirst down the narrow flight of uncarpeted stairs. He lay in an unconscious heap at the bottom, his head nearly touching the door. His eyes were closed and their long lashes cast feathery shadows on a face so pale that for a moment my grandmother had thought he was dead.

Her anguished scream tore through the paper-thin walls of the tiny terrace house and brought the neighbours running. In those days there were no telephones in the impoverished districts of Coleraine and no means of summoning an ambulance urgently. A neighbour's son was hastily sent running to the doctor's house and precious minutes were wasted before the doctor arrived. The boy was carefully lifted up, placed on the back seat of the doctor's old car and driven to the nearest hospital with his frantic mother.

Several weeks were to pass before the family was reassured he was out of danger.

During that time, my grandmother visited him every day. Heavily pregnant, a shawl thrown over her shoulders for warmth, a long black skirt rubbing the tops of her scuffed boots, she made the journey across town, never minding rain or cold. Once there, she would sit at her auburn-haired son's bedside, praying for his life. She gave birth to her fourth child during that harrowing time – another boy and her last child. No sooner had she recovered from her confinement, than her daily walk recommenced and she took up her vigil at her son's bedside.

My grandmother remembered vividly the day his eyes opened and he saw her and gave a faint smile. Years later, her eyes would still mist over when she recollected that moment. Joe recovered his health but for months was unable to speak. When he finally managed a few words it was with a stutter so bad that his face would redden from the exertion of forcing out the syllables.

It was thirty years before a welfare state and work in Belfast was scarce. My grandfather, a cobbler, worked long hours in the tiny back room of his house repairing shoes. With small children, a baby and two adults to feed, money was scarce and there was little left over to pay medical bills for his eldest. Life was a daily struggle and money for a private tutor to bring Joe back up to the standard at school he had been before the accident was an unheard of luxury. Neither parent had the education themselves to help. Instead one year later he returned to the local school, behind with his schoolwork and with a noticeable speech impediment. At the age of nine he was placed in the same class he had left – the one for eight-year-olds.

Tall for his age, he towered above the other children. They thought he was an easy target and made the mistake of teasing him – and teasing was something that my father simply could not tolerate. He responded with aggression and his popularity waned.

His mood changed and the previously happy little boy disappeared.

My grandmother knew he was unhappy at the school but there was little she could do. It was then that his sudden rages started. With a growl, he would leap at his persecutors, his fists drawn back and, with all the strength he possessed, he would let fly until his tormentor was on the ground. The other children quickly learnt not to tease him and to be wary of his fists.

It was not until Joe became an adult that he learned how to make people like him again.

I thought about the parallel lines my childhood and his had run on. I was damaged in a different way, unable to express myself and seen as an outsider. I was also bullied at school but unlike him I never fought back. As a child, I had watched the world as though through a sheet of glass. I had never felt part of it and, as I became older, making friends scared me. I could not identify with other children so what could I talk to them about?

He too must have felt apart from his contemporaries. He must have watched his schoolmates playing and laughing, and felt separated from them. Whereas I had tried to mimic mine, he couldn't. Loneliness for me resulted in further isolation and depression. For him, it became rage and bitterness.

In my father's mind, nothing was ever his fault; it was always someone else's. Every wrong action could be justified, every selfish deed excused. Seeds which might have lain dormant took root and grew into something dark and twisted. My father chose to take a different route from me.

For a moment I felt sad as I recalled my father when he was a young man and I had loved him. But the memories of the man he was as I grew up quickly obliterated any others, the one who had inspired such deep fear that the only way to cope with it was to shut down completely.

I thought of the last few days I had spent in Larne and of the last time I had seen my father alive. I had caught the shuttle service to Belfast after social services had contacted me to say he had been admitted to hospital after a mild stroke followed by pneumonia. If I wanted to see him before he died, there was little time to spare. Far from understanding my own actions, I had booked the morning flight, gone to the hospital and asked for directions to my father's ward. With every step, I asked myself why I had come. Why had I caught that plane from London to Belfast? Why should I want to see him?

Finding his ward, I pushed open the swing doors and entered a room where old men lay dozing in their metal beds. I saw my father. In preparation for my visit, he had been dressed in clean pyjamas, wrapped in a wool dressing gown and, with freshly combed hair, had been placed in an upright arm chair beside his bed. I could see that he had only a short time to live. Approaching death had stripped him of his power and reduced him to a form that appeared peculiarly boneless. His mouth hung slackly open; drool had gathered in the corners and escaping flecks had left damp tracks on his chin. Rheumy eyes made misty by the onset of cataracts showed no recognition as they stared blankly into space.

All signs of that vital force that I remembered inhabiting his body were gone. My father, the tyrant of my childhood, the man who had sexually abused me at six and made me pregnant at fourteen, was dying.

Again I asked myself why I had come. Why was I standing at the foot of this bed? Why had I walked back into that other life which came complete with its torment? Standing there with an overnight suitcase at my feet, I told myself that no one deserves to die alone. But the truth was that the invisible shackles of our blood tie had drawn me back for the last time.

My father's frail old man's body shocked me. The faded stripes of his pyjamas contrasted harshly with the red leatherette chair, a rug covered his knees and his sockless feet were tucked into green plaid slippers. Only one age-spotted hand grasping the corner of his rug and kneading it with his fingers showed that he was conscious. He moaned softly, still without giving any sign that he was aware of my presence, and I took his other hand. Looking closer to see the cause of his distress, I saw that ulcers had formed inside his mouth dotting that sensitive area with their small white blisters. I called the nurse.

'Please clean his mouth,' I told her as, with some annoyance, I pointed them out.

'He might have lost the power of speech but he can still feel pain.'

Seeing him now, so powerless to help himself, made the anger I had felt towards him for so many years, the anger I wanted to hold on to, shrivel and die within me. He's just an old man I told myself, as something akin to pity rose in its place.

Pulling up the second chair, I sat near him and studied the face which both age and sickness had rendered curiously expressionless. Wavy hair now turned white still covered his head thickly. His teeth had been removed, causing the cheeks to sink and the chin to drop. With that final indignity there was little to remind me of the charming charismatic man he had once been to the people who saw his public face. And there was no sign of the monster that had tormented me for so many years.

I remembered being told by the nurses at the hospice where my mother had died that the last of the senses to go is hearing but I had no words for him. For this parent, there were no last thoughts I wanted to share and neither were there memories I wanted to bring alive for him to take on that final journey.

Did he even know I was there? I wondered, as the minutes became hours which ticked away silently and slowly. Reaching into my bag, I took out a book which served as a shield to hide behind, a trick I'd learnt as a child when I wanted to escape the anger of my parents' voices. But try as I might to prevent them, images of my father as a younger man floated in front of my eyes. Pictures of the smiling handsome man who many years ago I had loved came uninvited into my mind. I willed myself not to look at them but no sooner were they banished than another memory followed; that of the man with the bloodshot eyes and mouth that quivered in rage at any imaginary wrong. I saw Antoinette the child cower and once again felt her fear.

The nurse came to my side as dusk fell. 'Toni, go home and rest. This could last for several days. We'll call you if anything changes.'

Not knowing what my father had been, she gave my shoulder a compassionate squeeze.

I went not to his home with its old-man smell of stale air and unwashed bedding, but to a friend's house where a spare bedroom had been made ready. Supper was waiting when I arrived but all I wanted was to go to the privacy of my room. There I felt I could crawl into the welcoming bed and switch off from the world. Once alone, I could force my mind to centre on pleasant thoughts that would barricade me from the past. It was a ploy I'd perfected over the years.

So tired was I from the day's events that no sooner had my head touched the pillow than I fell into a deep dreamless sleep. It seemed that only minutes passed before the ringing of the phone forced me unwillingly awake. Knowing already that the call was for me, I wearily reached for the extension phone placed by the bed.

'Your father's taken a turn for the worse,' said the ward sister. 'You'd better come.'

I dressed hurriedly, pulling on a warm tracksuit and slipping my feet into trainers, then went to alert my friends. They were ready for me, the husband in the car running the engine to warm it, for they knew the ringing of the phone in the early hours of that cold morning could only mean one thing.

We were silent on the short drive to the hospital. I knew that closure of a kind was happening but the knowledge brought mixed feelings. Soon, the only person left responsible for bringing me into the world would be dead and the death of the remaining parent makes us aware of our own mortality. There is no one left who sees us as a child, and that alone creates a feeling of vulnerability. And I knew that with him would die answers to the questions I had never had the courage to ask.

Our arrival in the ward was greeted by the eerie silence that lingers for a few minutes as the soul departs.

My father had died alone after all.

Chapter Twenty-Nine

The short journey from the psychiatric ward to the main building passed in silence. Antoinette, bundled in the back of the ambulance, sat shivering more with fear than with cold as she stared blankly out of the window.

The ambulance drew up in front of the building; the doors opened, the orderly leaned in and she felt her arm being taken.

'We're here, Antoinette,' said one of her escorts.

Still without speaking, she climbed out of the vehicle. The two male nurses walked on either side of her as they led her through the massive wooden doors into the main building. The ever-pervading smell of a badly ventilated old building hung in the air as they walked down cheerless, grey-floored corridors. Their monotony was broken only by dark wooden doors that led into the secured female wards.

There was no sign that any effort had been made to improve the building since its transformation from poorhouse to mental hospital. Nothing had been done to soften its austerity – there were no potted plants or pictures on the walls. Nothing relieved the long corridors that stretched for yards upon yards; they were as grim then as they must have been in Victorian times when the destitute had first occupied the place.

Only the faint sound of her escorts' shoes broke the eerie silence that hung over the sleeping building. Antoinette hardly heard it as she concentrated on counting the doors that led to the female wards until she knew they had arrived at F3A.

As soon as the guard knocked lightly on the door, it swung open. The night sister in charge had obviously been waiting for them and no sooner had she ushered Antoinette in than the door was closed firmly behind her. She heard the rattle of the keys and then the click as the lock turned – and she knew that it was the sound of her being separated from freedom.

Events had moved so fast that Antoinette had barely enough time to take in what was happening to her. She had a fleeting impression of dark walls, small, high-set barred windows and hard concrete flooring before the night sister touched her gently on the arm and indicated that she was to follow her.

She quickly led Antoinette to the dormitory. Following in her wake, Antoinette clutched her few possessions and felt her fear intensify. If the sister noticed, she gave no response. To her, Antoinette was just another patient transferred at night, to be put to bed as quickly as possible.

'Don't make a noise. The other patients are sleeping,' she said as they entered another room where dim lights cast shadows over rows of sleeping forms huddled in narrow metal beds.

Without curtains pulled around them to preserve a semblance of dignity, the inmates had no illusions of having their own room. Instead the beds were close together with only a small metal locker separating each from its neighbour.

The nurse stopped at one covered with a grey blanket. 'That's your bed,' she said. 'I'll put your case under it and you can sort your things out in the morning. Just take out your nightdress for now.'

Antoinette felt her skin prickle as goosebumps rose on her arms and she hastily pulled off her clothes and replaced them with her pyjamas. When she was finished, the sister took her to the washrooms. Large white baths stood in the centre of a room; at the side of each was a small wooden chair. Against one wall were uncurtained tiled showers where black hosepipes hung, coiled like slumbering snakes. She had heard about the hosepipes and how they were used on the patients by the orderlies: after stripping, the naked women were herded into the open showers and hosed down with cold water. This served two purposes – it subdued the unruly ones and bathed the lot of them all the quicker.

Next to the showers were rows of wash basins and on the opposite wall were the toilets. She looked at their doors with mounting dismay and when she went inside the cubicle, her fears were justified: they hardly hid her. They stopped at her knees and the top was cut so low that her head could be seen when standing, and there was no way of closing them firmly as there were no locks. Antoinette realized that even the most private part of life would be observed.

It was not until she climbed into her bed that the reality of where she was finally penetrated her consciousness. Now waves of anxiety rolled over her and her hands grew clammy as they clutched the bedclothes for comfort. Feelings of bewildered abandonment were threatening to overcome her. Surely her parents must know what had happened to her. They couldn't let her stay here, could they? Even if they did not love her, they could not hate her that much. Round and round the thoughts scurried in her brain, making it impossible to sleep.

In the gloom, she could make out the indistinct shapes of the other women all around her, hear their deep breathing and their childlike cries as they tossed in their sleep. The sound of grinding teeth came from a nearby bed, snores punctuated by mutterings from another. Antoinette lay with her eyes wide open, wondering what the following day would bring.

Morning came and with it the noise of the day staff arriving. Antoinette rose, collected her clothes and took herself to the washrooms. She wanted to use them before the other patients got up, feeling it was her only chance of preserving her privacy. She hurriedly washed, put on the same clothes she had been wearing the night before, and then returned to her bed.

Knowing that the nurses disliked having to straighten the bedclothes of physically healthy people, she quickly made hers and then sat on the end of it, waiting to be told what to do. She did not have to wait too long. The ward sister sent a young nurse to fetch her.

'Sister wants you to come with me,' she said shortly, without pausing for introductions. 'She's waiting for you.'

Only a few yards separated the dormitory from the ward sister's office. They passed through a large room where the patients spent their days. It was bleak, with basic wooden furniture and barred windows, but Antoinette barely noticed. All she registered was the jangling of the large bunch of keys that hung from the nurse's belt, and the ceaseless babble of background noise coming from the patients with its low note of desolation. Later, she would not only see the grim bareness of her surroundings, she would also feel the hopelessness and the raw despair that permeated the atmosphere.

Entering the small room which served as the sister's office, Antoinette noticed its internal windows gave a clear view of the ward and the desk inside was positioned so that the ward sister could watch the activities in it. The sister, a small dark-haired woman, was sitting at her desk and she rose up to greet Antoinette as she came in.

'Hello, you must be Antoinette,' she said pleasantly. 'Please, take a seat.'

Antoinette was surprised. She had been expecting at least some degree of sternness and was taken aback by the sister's open, friendly face and kindly smile.

The sister pointed to the tray with teapot and two cups. 'Do you take milk and sugar?'

Antoinette nodded, not trusting herself to speak, and watched as the sister poured out a cup of tea for each of them. She murmured 'Thank you' when it was given to her, and curled her fingers round the cup, taking comfort from its warmth. She waited apprehensively for the sister to begin. Now, surely, she would learn her fate.

After a short pause, the sister said gravely, 'Antoinette, what do you know about this ward?' Without waiting for an answer, she continued, 'This is not a place where people get the same treatment as you received where you were before. This is where patients are tranquillized if they cause trouble. We do not have the allocation of staff here to be able to cope if we did not do that. Do you understand?'

Antoinette understood. She recognized that a warning, carefully wrapped and prettily presented, had just been given. She said nothing.

The ward sister opened a brown folder, the only one on her desk, and Antoinette realized that it was her case history.

'Should the women here become uncontrollable, they are given electric shock treatment.' The sister sighed wearily. 'We try and look after them as best as we can. Hardly any patients here receive visitors and they are beyond the help of therapy. But in your case, I've arranged for you to see a psychiatrist weekly. From your notes, it seems that you were beginning to respond to the one you were seeing on the psychiatric wing but unfortunately she does not treat patients in the main building. I also see from your file that you were uncooperative with the senior psychiatrist who assessed you. Well, the one I have arranged for you to see is also a man, if that was the reason you found it difficult, but I think you will like him.'

Antoinette looked at her directly at this last comment. Did this mean that in some way this woman wanted to help her?

The sister ignored the questioning look and continued, 'The only time patients leave this ward is when they are taken to the dining room for meals. There they eat in a separate section so there is no mixing with the other wards. The rest of the time, apart from when they are sleeping, they stay in the communal room you have just walked through. Did you notice the locked chairs?'

Antoinette nodded. The sister meant the wooden chairs that were fitted with a small table that locked into place and stopped a patient from moving about. For a moment, she had the impression that the lack of expression in the ward sister's voice covered up feelings of disquiet at some of the treatment given in those wards.

'Some of our patients spend nearly all their time in them. You might find that sight distressing and think it's cruel – but we're not being unkind to them, you know. Some of the women here were born with problems and have the mental age of a toddler but the strength of an adult. If they were not restricted, they could hurt each other as well as themselves. Some have been so damaged that long ago we knew they would never recover. They would never be capable of coping with the outside world. There are others who are dangerous. Two have been sectioned for murder. The more normal they seem, the more dangerous they are. So you will have to be careful of them. They have attacked nurses and other patients.' She paused for breath and gave Antoinette a reflective look. 'Others, like you, have simply not been able to cope with the tragedy of their lives.'

Now Antoinette felt the whole point of this interview was going to be revealed. A small glimmer of hope flickered in her. Surely this woman would not be so nice to her if she felt there was no hope for her? Perhaps things were not as bleak as she had feared.

The ward sister sighed and closed the folder. 'I've read your file and your case is a tragic one. But there are so many sad stories we hear in this place and yours is just one of them, even if to you it is everything. I believe that when you are able to realize that there are people who have suffered even more than you, you will start to get better. I know it is too soon for you to accept that but I hope that you are going to be one of my success stories.'

Antoinette blinked in surprise – nobody had ever said that to her before. Still she said nothing.

'Don't worry about the locked chairs. They're for the worst cases, not for you. There is absolutely no reason for you to be restrained in one and I hope you never give us one.' And again Antoinette felt the warning underneath the reassurance. 'Now, the treatment that has been recommended for you is a course of Paraldehyde, to be taken in liquid form.'

The fear came back again. Antoinette had seen the effects of those heavy drugs and she dreaded them. Visions of the convoys of shuffling inmates with blank faces and downcast eyes sprung into her mind and her hands clutched the tea cup tighter. Nothing except excessive doses of electric shock treatment could turn someone into a zombie quicker, and zombies did not recover.

The sister saw her alarm and quickly continued, 'However, the psychiatric ward can only recommend treatment given in this section of the hospital. I have insisted that you are first placed under observation and assessed by one of our psychiatrists.' She smiled. 'You have been diagnosed as suffering from acute paranoia. The sister from your last unit has stated in her report that you attacked a patient who gave you no provocation. In her opinion, you are dangerous. Well, that is her opinion. I have to form my own.'

Antoinette began to relax. Although she had learned never to trust anyone in a position of authority, she was feeling more at ease with this woman. Despite her veiled warnings, she appeared to be on her side. The fact that she would not begin the doses of Paraldehyde that the ward sister had decreed seemed to offer Antoinette a chance.

'It is imperative that you co-operate both with my team and with the psychiatrist I will arrange for you to meet,' the sister said finally as she concluded the meeting. She rose and, telling Antoinette to follow her, led the way into the unit's main room.

As they went, Antoinette wished she had been able to say something to explain herself and to reassure the ward sister that she did not need to be tranquillized into submission, but she had been unable to find her voice. It had been the same with the psychiatrists in the other ward. She had longed to be able to tell them more but so much was in a tangle locked within her head. Inside, there were suppressed memories that she was too scared to look at and thoughts and feelings that were too awful to put into words. There were the days when she simply could not release the words necessary to communicate even the most basic idea, let alone the trauma of her past.

It was that inability that had given the ward sister a free hand when she wrote that report.

Chapter Thirty

A ntoinette stood in the room, surrounded by women who showed no interest in the arrival of a new patient, trying to take in her surroundings. Dirty green paint covered the walls and the windows, whose black-painted bars she had seen from the grounds outside, were set well above head height. In one corner were two comfortable chairs with cushions – those were for the nurses on duty. The rest of the unoccupied seats were of dark, hard wood with no concession to comfort.

The room was full of women, patients from whom all traces of individuality had been drained away. Dressed in the hospital uniform of shapeless faded paisley dresses and grey cardigans, the inmates wore the expressionless look of the heavily sedated. Some were muttering to themselves while others just stared mutely at the bare walls. Antoinette felt her eyes widen in shock as she realized that nearly every one of these women were locked into a chair. It was the first time she had seen these contraptions in use and the sight of them revolted her.

At first glance, they looked like any other wooden chair with arms and a small shelf that doubled up as a table, but when those trays were locked into place, the person sitting inside was trapped, with only their arms free.

But these are human beings, she thought, appalled, as she saw how many women were imprisoned where they sat, unable to stand up or walk. Humans who are ill. It can't be right to treat them like this.

Some patients sat quietly in their chairs, others rocked with so much force that they pushed their chairs backwards and forwards as they did so. Some who were not locked into place crouched against walls, their hands covering their eyes, lost in a fear that Antoinette recognized without understanding why.

The sound of wood knocking against walls or bouncing on the floors combined with the continuous babble of senseless words, moans and shrieks was so full of hopeless misery that Antoinette recoiled.

She pulled herself together before she gave away the horror she felt. She did not want the nurses to see her feelings reflected on her face. She wanted to be as unobtrusive as possible. Taking a book from her bag, she sat on one of the chairs and put her head down, trying to look fully absorbed. She found that she had read a page without remembering one word and again looked round the room.

Her eyes were drawn to a girl who looked to be no more than thirteen years old. Locked into one of the chairs, she lolled over its wooden arm, lank hair hanging around a face devoid of all expression. Her tongue protruded from a loose mouth while her glazed eyes stared unseeingly at the floor.

At that moment, one of the nurses went over to her and said in cheerful tones, 'Time for your walk, Mary.'

Where are they taking her, wondered Antoinette. She watched the nurse unlock the wooden tray, put her arms under the girl's shoulders and heave her into a standing position. Mary set off across the room, her eyes still staring at the floor but her legs moving in a jerky rhythm. She tottered along until she hit the wall on the far side, but that did not deter her. She kept walking, going nowhere, her body knocking on the plaster until another nurse pulled herself out of her chair, walked leisurely over and turned her around, setting her off towards the other side. Mary's walk was twenty minutes of crossing a room over and over again. Once the nurses were bored with the effort of turning her around, they placed her back in her chair. There she lolled over the arm again and resumed staring blankly at the floor.

Mary was so young – what had happened to her? Why was a girl who was scarcely more than a child in a place like this? Antoinette found out later that the girl had been a victim of meningitis. Once a bright child, she had contacted the virus when she was eleven. There was little treatment and nearly all who caught it died. Mary survived but with permanent and irreversible brain damage. When her parents had realized the dedication required to look after a handicapped daughter, they had signed the consent forms to have her admitted to the hospital. She had been there for two years and without individual attention or even having one person visit her, she had deteriorated to such a degree that she would never leave. Now she was incapable of recognizing anyone.

Antoinette felt an overpowering pity at the sight of that skinny form imprisoned in a chair; a forgotten girl who once had run and played and never would again.

A voice broke into her thoughts. It was a woman asking, 'Don't you love my baby?'

She looked up and saw a small woman with the face of a fifty-year-old and the guileless smile of a child. In her arms she cradled a doll which she was holding up for Antoinette's

inspection. 'Don't you love my baby?' she asked again, looking at her intently.

'Yes, she's very beautiful. What's her name?' She smiled
back. She couldn't help responding to such a childlike person
and the large blue eyes that looked at her so hopefully.

The little woman beamed back and then trotted off to ask
the same question of someone else.

'She lost her baby a long time ago,' muttered one of the
nurses. 'Her name's Doris. She's no trouble. She never says
anything except that. A hundred times a day or more.'

'What happened to her?' asked Antoinette timidly. She
wasn't sure whether it was the done thing to ask about other
patients' histories, or whether the nurses were allowed to tell
what they knew. It didn't seem to bother this one. She seemed
glad of someone she could hold a reasonable conversation with.

'Oh, I don't think Doris was ever the brightest of sparks,'
she said with a shrug. 'She got herself pregnant, anyway,
when she wasn't married. So they put her in a home for
unmarried mothers and took her baby boy from her when he
was six weeks old. She got very down after that – you know,
depressed – and in the end, she shut herself off completely so
her family seized their chance, signed the papers and had her
committed.'

'Was she always like this?'

'Not at first. But she's had electric shock treatment and she
takes the medicine that keeps her calm and quiet. It's been ten
years now that she's been here and she'll never leave.' The
nurse looked at Antoinette warily. 'But she's not unhappy, you
can see that. And she's got what she wanted. Her baby's with
her all the time now, isn't he?'

Antoinette tried to hide her shock. She had seen many
patients with little wrong with them living in the hospital but

this was the first time she had been so close to people who had been destroyed by lack of treatment and abandonment.

She resolved that she was not going to lose herself in this ward.

Chapter Thirty-One

Antoinette looked at the small pile of clothing which had been placed at the foot of her bed: a print dress of faded dark maroon, a shapeless fawn cardigan, baggy knickers with suspenders attached and a vest. Beside them lay thick brown lisle stockings, a wincyette nightdress and a pair of scuffed, well-worn, lace-up black shoes.

'Your clothes,' the nurse told her.

'But I have my own.' The thought of wearing the hospital uniform which had covered so many bodies was abhorrent to her. The distinctive smell of cheap soap mixed with the musty smell of the unaired laundry where the racks of washing dried repelled her. And somehow she knew that in giving up wearing her own clothes she would be giving up her own identity. She would join the world of vacant-eyed women whose days were spent rocking backwards and forwards in their chairs as they hummed tunelessly to the music in their heads, or become one of those who only heard the ghosts of their past. Some of them talked to their ghosts in a language that was theirs alone, and sometimes the ghosts induced anger – shouts, curses and plates of food hurled into the air.

The uniform would mean she was one of them. It would dehumanize her and turn her into just another face in a crowd of people who had been robbed of their individuality and become little more than animals to those who cared for them. That's what it represented to the nurses who stripped the women of their clothes and herded them naked into communal showers where, without a vestige of dignity, they were hosed down. The nurses did not see the women in their care as people who had once had desires and hopes. There was no trace of empathy on their faces when they distributed the drugs which took away life and thought and dreams, or stood by when electric shock was given.

Antoinette thought of the thirteen-year-old Mary and saw her tottering pathetically from wall to wall. The only time she was ever noticed was when the nurses dragged themselves from their chairs and turned her round. But if she were dressed in the clothes of a normal girl, with her hair neatly braided and her face washed, and if she hadn't been made dull eyed by the onslaught of the drugs, would the profession that prided itself on kindness have treated her like a rag doll? Or would they seen have an abandoned child?

Antoinette knew what the uniform meant. It was the first step to a lifetime in this place. It was the first admission of defeat.

'I have my own clothes,' she insisted, coming out of her reverie.

'I know you have but who's going to wash them? That's why we have hospital clothes – so you can have clean ones every week.'

Still she stood refusing to touch the pile on the bed.

'Antoinette,' the nurse said patiently, 'people in the ward you came from get visitors but nobody here does. So what does it matter what you wear? And here you have someone to take your clothes away and bring them back all clean and nicely folded, so I don't see what there is to complain about.'

'I'll wash them myself.' With those words, she turned away. She knew she could not hold out for ever but she was not ready to become one of the lost souls who lived inside this strange other country, separated from the outside by walls of prejudice and indifference.

Chapter Thirty-Two

The sister arranged for her to have books to read. Antoinette found that her concentration was beginning to return and she enjoyed being able to read again. She returned to her childhood favourites, starting with the mysteries of Agatha Christie. She had not read any of them since she was thirteen and now there was a comfort from their familiarity.

During the long days in the communal room, she would settle herself as comfortably as possible on one of the hard wooden chairs and lose herself in her book.

Two women, one no more than twenty and the other five or six years older, were always together and she knew they were convicted murderers. She noticed that, unlike the other patients, they could hold a conversation and, when she couldn't read any more, Antoinette was desperate for some company. Apart from the nurses and the one session she had a week with her psychiatrist, she was starved of human contact. But so far, neither woman had approached her; they did not seem to want any other company and sat huddled together, ignoring the other patients. Antoinette wondered what she could do to attract their attention and make them want to mix with her.

There was no entertainment in the room except for an old television which the nurses commandeered. Antoinette had brought two packs of cards with her and one day, feeling more eager than ever for some company, she decided to use them to tempt the women into wanting to play with her. She put her plan into action by pulling up a chair near them and shuffling the cards for a game of patience.

From the corner of her eye, she saw that she had got their attention and before long, the elder of the two women approached her. 'What's that you're doing?'

'Playing solo. Do you play cards?' she asked carefully.

'No. Don't know how,' was the grudging answer.

'I could teach you, and your friend – if you'd like to,' she offered casually, hoping that the other woman would bite at the line she had so carefully baited.

The woman thought for a moment and then said, 'All right. We'll join you.'

From then on, every evening the two women and Antoinette formed a trio. After supper the cards would appear and Antoinette taught them the games she had learnt from her English grandmother. She wondered where her grandmother thought she was living these days. What explanations had Ruth given to her of what her daughter was doing with her life? No doubt she was saying that Antoinette was giving her trouble but that she was bravely coping, she thought wryly. But it hurt to think of her family and she pushed them firmly out of her mind.

Routine was important to Antoinette and gradually she found her life in the main building settle into a comfortable rhythm. She was not happy but the clouds of her black depression had lifted, leaving in their place a placidity that made her content with very little.

She found that the nurses were almost motherly to her, taking pleasure in her gradual return to normality. It seemed that she was a rarity. In these wards, people were not expected to improve and they hardly ever did. The nurses were more like guards than carers and seeing a patient begin to recover gave them a feeling of accomplishment. Antoinette was aware of this and tried even harder to please them, for she was still just a teenager who craved approval. She could not help thinking that all the nurses were sure that she should not be there and that helping her along the path to recovery had become a challenge. She was aware that she was being treated differently.

Although they were kind to her, she sometimes thought that the team of nurses was trying to trick her into saying she wanted to leave by asking questions such as 'Is England a place you would like to visit?' or 'Will you see your grandmother when you are there?' She knew that they were trying to make her admit that there was a future for her beyond this place but it was not something she was ready to consider. The future was something that she had blocked out of her mind; she was still too busy with dealing with her past and coping with her present. So she never answered their questions but only smiled.

After her refusal to wear the hospital uniform there was no more mention made of her having to conform. Instead, she washed her clothes herself and a couple of times a week she was taken to the hospital laundry where she was allowed to iron them. She had worried that wearing her own clothes would make her look different to everyone else, as though she was trying to set herself above them, but no one appeared to notice. Even her card-playing friends, who she thought might object to a privilege they didn't have, did not seem to mind. They had lost the desire to wear their own clothes. Why spend all that time washing and ironing them, they said, when our uniforms are done for us? The older one pointed out there were no men to attract so who would see them anyway?

Antoinette did not tell them that she did it to remind herself who she was.

Although she still had to be observed and have daily reports written about her, the nurses did not appear to believe the ward sister's report that she was a threat to the other patients. In such a ward, however, caution was always exercised and she was not allowed to leave the room without an escort.

Antoinette's two friends, her fellow card players, did not seem like murderers but Antoinette had been warned to stay vigilant. It was the elder, Elaine, who was really dangerous, the nurses said, and after looking into the cold depths of her eyes, Antoinette believed it.

Elaine, Antoinette was told, was a double murderer. She had killed two members of her family in cold blood. Not only had she never given an explanation of why she had done it – except that they had annoyed her – she had never shown any remorse. Antoinette believed that the annoyance she had felt was the explanation. Before she had arrived on ward F3A, Elaine had stood on a chair, pushed her fist through the bars and smashed a window. Snatching up a shard of glass, she had jumped down and held it to the throat of a nurse, laughing as she did it. The alarms had rung, male orderlies had appeared and eventually she had been persuaded to relinquish her weapon and let the nurse go. She had been given tranquillizers followed by electric shock treatment but there was still something about her bearing that warned of impending aggression.

The younger girl, Jenny, with her mop of dark auburn curls and blue eyes, looked more sad than violent, Antoinette thought. Jenny seemed intimidated by Elaine who watched her every move but until Antoinette arrived, they were the only two women in the ward who could relate to one another and that had made them cling together.

Antoinette knew that it was not the desire for her company but their enjoyment of playing cards that made them mix with her but she also acknowledged it was only boredom that made her seek out theirs. A week after they starting playing, the three received an unexpected bonus. Nurses on night duty get bored too and now the evenings were spent with five women playing the games Antoinette taught them and in return she bargained for pots of tea and permission to stay up later. The women played for counters made out of paper and Antoinette, who was the better player, had the sense to allow Elaine to win at least once a night.

Entering the sitting area of the ward one day, after she had returned from her session with her psychiatrist, Antoinette found Jenny sitting dejectedly by herself. During the nights they had sat together, the younger woman had roused her curiosity. Unlike Elaine, there was nothing about her that gave any indication of repressed violence. She had seen Elaine shaking with rage and once she had flown into a temper and two nurses had struggled to control her. But Jenny seemed harmless.

Antoinette crossed the room to take a seat by her. 'Where's Elaine?' she asked. It was seldom that Jenny was alone; the older woman seemed a permanent fixture at her side.

'She's got bad stomach cramps and they've put her in a side ward to rest. The doctor's coming to see her later.'

'I'm sorry to hear that. I hope she'll be all right.'

Jenny shrugged indifferently and continued to stare sadly into space. Antoinette sat quietly waiting for her to speak, and after a few minutes, she said, 'You know, I'll never leave this place.'

Antoinette didn't know what to say. She only allowed herself to think of one day at a time and never thought of being released. Her only ambition for the future was that she hoped to be transferred back to the psychiatric ward. Besides, not only did she hear the note of bleak acceptance in Jenny's voice but she'd also been told that by the nurses that Jenny was almost certainly in here for life. Eventually she plucked up the courage to say timidly, 'But what did you do?'

'I killed a baby,' was the bald reply.

Antoinette flinched and, seeing her recoil, Jenny put her head in her hands.

'I didn't mean to. It was an accident. But nobody believed me. I was only fifteen years old then. My mother worked for these people and so did my dad. He was the gardener, me mom the housekeeper and they had been given a cottage. Part of their wages it was. It was damp and the owners never did it up even though they had loads of money. They were a snotty couple – always going out and asking me to watch their baby. They left her with me one night when she must have been teething and she just wouldn't shut up. You know what babies are like once they get started – they can scream and holler for hours. Well, in the end, I was in that much of a temper that I picked her up and shook her, and I shook her too hard. Her neck broke. It was terrible and even though I said it was an accident and I hadn't meant it, there was a huge fuss and commotion and they called the police. Me mum cried and screamed, me father beat me. They all said I was a murderer and then they put me in here. They turned my mum and dad and my brothers and sisters out of their cottage anyhow. I've not seen any of them since. I don't even know where they are now.'

'How long have you been here?'

'Four years and I miss my family every day. You know, I'm not the same as Elaine.'

Antoinette knew she wasn't. She saw the double tragedy: a life that had been snuffed out and one that was wasted. Pity stirred in her. Then she pictured a tiny baby being shaken so hard that its fragile neck snapped and she found it impossible to comfort Jenny. Instead she said, 'Let's play a game of cards, shall we?'

Antoinette shuffled and dealt but her heart was not in it. Jenny was the same age as she was and surely she deserved a second chance. But the chances that she would ever leave were slim. The best she had to look forward to was a transfer to the one of the unlocked wards, and that was only when the authorities were sure that she had become too institutionalized to attempt an escape.

Antoinette was beginning to realize that failure to recover meant becoming a permanent resident of the strange world that existed inside the hospital.

Even in the psychiatric ward, she had seen people arrive searching for a cure to their problems, only to find that the 'cure' condemned them to a lifetime inside this place.

She thought of two people, a slim pretty girl in her late teens and a young man not much older, who had been admitted to hospital with the same problem – addiction to alcohol. They had not known each other but they both came from families of strict Methodists, who saw their illness as a sin.

The two of them had met in the unit and been drawn together by their common bond – their desire to overcome their alcoholism.

Antoinette had seen them sitting together in the lounge, their heads close together as they talked quietly, not needing any company but their own. Other times she had seen them walking in the grounds, their hands almost but not quite touching. Patients in the psychiatric ward were allowed to mix freely and it was obvious to everyone that these two had fallen in love.

Fired with the belief that the depth of feeling they had for each other had cured them, they signed themselves out against their doctor's wishes. They were going to start a new life together, the couple told everyone, and with good wishes from everyone for their future, they left.

Two months later they returned, their skin yellow, their eyes aged and their hopes dashed. Their new life had taken them straight to a pub. Just one drink to celebrate our release, they had told each other. Just another because we are cured, then another and another until they forgot about their cure and what they were celebrating.

This time round they were given treatment that was designed to save them. In the twenty-first century it would be classed as torture. They were locked for three days and nights in separate side wards. Nourishing food was withheld. Instead, they were given whiskey. When they weakly pushed it aside, it was held to their mouths and poured down their throats. When raging thirsts awoke them, instead of the cool refreshing water that now they craved, more whiskey was given. Pills were washed down by the liquid which had become their worst enemy, pills that made their bodies heave with the effort of spewing the force-fed liquor out. Their bodies convulsed again and again as the whiskey mixed with burning bile rose up their throats and spewed from their mouths in hot gushes to splatter on to the floor where it remained for the three days of their 'cure'.

The nurse who told Antoinette what she had seen described how the rooms stank with vomit. As the patients grew too weak to lean out of their beds, it made pools in their bedding, clung in lumps to their hair and filled everything with the stench.

When it was over, they no longer loved whiskey and their sense of dignity and self-respect had been destroyed. Once again the couple was discharged but this time they drank vodka. They might be able to replace the whiskey but nothing could ever replace their feelings of self-worth. Alcohol deadened their grief of its loss until once again they were returned and another 'cure' administered.

Eventually, they gave up their fight to live in the world outside. They now were in separate wards for long-stay patients. It had not been deemed necessary to place them in locked ones. They had nowhere left to run to. Antoinette had seen them wandering in the grounds, but never together. They were two lonely lost people whose sickness had drawn them together but whose cure had driven them apart.

Once she had wondered what would happen to them, and now she realized that nothing would. This was where their lives had ended.

Then there was the pretty red-haired woman she had met during her first stay. She had been sitting on a chair that had been placed outside her ward, warming herself in the sunshine. Antoinette remembered her when she was a woman who had been loved by a husband and her two children. She had seen the family visiting her and seen the bewilderment on the faces of the two little ones, who were too young to understand that their mother was ill and just wanted her to return home with them. But they wanted the mother they had known, not the one whose post-natal depression was so severe that she was lost to them.

Antoinette had heard that the husband had remarried and the two children no longer visited. Now the woman sat in a wooden chair, bent almost double, her prettiness long gone as the drugs that quietened her made her gums recede and her once-vibrant hair fade and thin.

In her twilight world that she had entered long ago, did she remember who she had once been, Antoinette wondered. She hoped not.

No, she thought. Once in this place we do not believe we will ever return to the outside world. Then the words of the sister came into her head. 'There are so many sad stories we hear in this place ... but I hope you are going to be one of my success stories.'

She looked up at the window where only a patch of sky showed. The outside world had receded and grown unreal.

After all, the sad stories had all started out there.

Chapter Thirty-Three

Breakfast was eaten in the ward. Lunch and the evening meal were taken in the huge canteen where plates of unappetizing stodgy food were served. Antoinette hated those escorted walks to the dining room. Once there, she and the inmates of the long-stay wards were separated from the other patients. Being part of the group that ate in a different part of the dining room marked her as being among the worst cases in the hospital and she was forced twice a day to see others' reactions to the inmates of her ward.

She knew she attracted stares as she walked along the corridors, the only one not in uniform, but with her head held high she ignored them. Her footsteps rang out amongst the shuffling of the others as she walked in front beside one of the nurses. Patients from other wards must think I'm very dangerous, she thought with some amusement.

When the ward sister sent for her, she wondered if she was going to be told she had to conform and wear a uniform like everyone else, but it seemed that the sister had seen her defiance for what it was: an aversion to the category that had been given to her.

'Now, Antoinette, I think that it would be good for you to work while you're in here,' she said without any preamble when Antoinette came into her office. 'Because you are in a secure ward, there have not been many places we could put you. But one of the wards is short staffed. Their care assistant has left. Would you like me to send you there in the daytime?' Before Antoinette could ask her any questions, she dangled the carrot she knew would prove irresistible. 'When you are there, you would sit with the nurses in the dining room. What do you think?'

Antoinette was too delighted at the thought of being occupied and escaping segregation in the canteen to ask what ward she would be sent to and the ward sister had sensibly kept that information to herself. All she could think of was no more detested walks to the dining hall and the privilege of having tea breaks with the staff. This would mean drinkable tea that hadn't stewed for hours in an urn, biscuits and some new company.

'Yes,' she replied promptly. 'I'll do it.'

'Good.' The ward sister smiled. 'You can start tomorrow.'

Antoinette went to bed that night wondering what work she would be given. All she had been told was that she would help the nurses with their bed making and cleaning.

It can't be too bad, she told herself. This is the worst ward of all of them, isn't it? So it can't be any more horrible than this.

The next morning she found out what she had agreed to.

She had barely finished her breakfast when a nurse appeared to take her the ward with a brisk 'Follow me, please'.

She walked obediently behind the nurse, who soon turned into a part of the hospital Antoinette had never been in before. It was silent at that hour in the morning; only when breakfast was over and cleared away would the army of female patients who cleaned the corridors appear.

They stopped outside a locked door. As the nurse put her key in the lock and opened it, a deafening noise was released from inside. A giant cacophony of sound reverberated, bounced off the walls and attacked her ears. It was a mixture of repetitive mutterings, screeches that rose in strength to a high-pitched crescendo and the shouts of meaningless words. Antoinette reeled from the sheer volume of it and the nurse grasped her arm firmly more to reassure than to restrain her.

No sooner had her ears become attuned to the clamour of the ward than she smelt a pungent stench so strong it made her eyes smart. She forced herself not to gag as her nostrils filled with the powerful odour of sweat, excrement and urine. The combined attack on her senses almost made her legs buckle as she took in her surroundings.

She had entered a travesty of a nursery. Here, instead of the very young, were the very old, who were nearing the end of their lives and were returning to an infantile state. It was filled with long metal cots in neat rows, their metal sides raised to stop their occupants jumping or falling out. Antoinette realized that some of the racket was not human but came from the metal bars of the cots being shaken by the wizened arms of the their occupants. Showing toothless gums, the women's faces contorted as they screamed and shouted incomprehensible sounds at the new arrivals.

The rows of cots contained the old of the hospital. Women in varying stages of decrepitude sat or lay in their beds. The weak sunlight from the windows shone on scalps pink through sparse white hair; nightdresses were drawn high on wrinkled legs, exposing nappies fastened round withered buttocks.

Some of these old women had regressed completely to the babies they had once been. Antoinette watched with horror as one explored the contents of her nappy with her bony fingers before smearing the bedclothes with her find. Others, most of them emaciated and wrinkled, crouched in their cots screaming obscenities from toothless mouths while they watched the newcomers with feral expressions.

This was where the long-stay patients came when they grew old. Most of them had minds that had never been repaired. They had lived in the hospital for the majority of their adult lives and for years had been fed a diet of sedatives while their brains had been subjected to excessive bolts of electricity. Now they were ending their days in that room, but not quietly.

For the first time Antoinette was made to confront what happened to patients who never left. She had not questioned the fact that during her time in the hospital she had never seen really old people, either in the wards she had been in or when she had caught glimpses of other inmates. But here was the answer to the question she had not asked herself. This is where patients were sent when their dementia became too disruptive. She shuddered, partly with revulsion and partly with an uneasy awareness that she could be looking at her own future.

Here, there was no remnant of human dignity left.

As she watched them, she wondered if any of them were mothers or grandmothers and then felt ashamed that she had been so disgusted at the sight of them. Whatever they were, they were still people. She remembered that the ward sister had told her that some of the patients had never progressed mentally beyond toddler stage, that some had been so damaged that their minds had snapped and could never be repaired. Antoinette understood how fear and frustration could damage the mind – years of that, along with the natural disintegration that age brings, would bring most people to this state. She felt a sudden sense of purpose. Whatever the reason was that had brought these old people here, they deserved their final months or even days to be eased as much as it was possible.

She looked at the nurses. Some of the staff there were not much older than she was. If they can work here, then so can I, Antoinette decided. Her first impulse on seeing the place had been to run back to the safety of her ward which now seemed like a haven of peace and tranquillity. She would not give in to it.

'Just imagine,' she told herself sternly, 'that these old ladies are two and entering the tantrum stage. You've cleaned up babies before – just tell yourself this is no different.'

She was aware that the nurse was looking at her, waiting for a horrified comment or an exclamation of repugnance and resolved not to give any.

'Where do you want me to start?' she asked.

The nurse looked at her with something approaching respect. 'You can work with the other care assistant,' she said and pointed down the ward to where Antoinette should go.

Mentally rolling up her sleeves, Antoinette found the other assistant, introduced herself and started work.

There were over twenty beds to make. Sheets covered with excrement had to be removed, rubber sheets wiped and fresh bedding tucked tightly in. All the time they worked, Antoinette was aware of old women, angry at being put out of their cots, glaring at them. When the last bed was finished, Antoinette straightened up with a grunt of satisfaction.

In this ward, her work as a mother's help in Butlins had stood her in good stead. When she had done one stint as a maid, she'd had to clean chalets when vomiting lager louts had missed the toilets and hit the floor. When she had worked as a chamber maid, she'd emptied chamber pots filled by men too lazy to leave their room to walk the short distance to the communal toilets. And when she had been a nanny, she had changed nappies, wiped nose, dressed wriggling bodies and coped with temper tantrums.

Still, nothing could have prepared Antoinette for this ward.

The care assistant looked at her with a smile. 'I think you've earned a cup of tea, Antoinette. We'll take a break now.'

Gratefully, she joined the small circle that made up the team who worked on the Senile Dementia Unit. Freshly made tea was poured, biscuits were passed round and she sat munching contentedly, feeling an easy-going acceptance from the others, the first she had known in months.

The nurses started explaining more about the patients. Most of them were doubly incontinent, they told her, while some were abusive, both verbally and physically.

If they're trying to frighten me, they won't succeed, she thought. Although she felt a flicker of doubt at being capable of doing anything at all, she asked calmly, 'What would you like me to do next?'

'Just help us and make yourself generally useful. We'll tell you what we need as we go along,' replied the staff nurse in charge of the group. Then she added with an encouraging smile, 'You seem to be doing all right so far.'

Antoinette helped clean up the floors, make beds and change the clothes of the occupants. In between the hours of back-breaking work, she tried to talk to some of the patients. She sat with the quieter ones and brushed their hair, finding that the gentle stroke of the brush coupled with the sound of her voice often soothed them. Sometimes she received a smile, sometimes a mouthful of obscenities.

She cringed away from other habits that so many of them had acquired. She had seen babies play with the contents of their nappies, using it like play dough. Here was the geriatric equivalent and it was certainly not cute or endearing, especially when they could not only spit and swear but throw the foul matter with surprising accuracy.

'All I want to know is,' Antoinette said despairingly to her fellow care assistant, 'why does their aim have to be so good when it comes to throwing stuff at us and so clumsy when they have food in the same hands?'

Her companion just smiled and wiped yet another wrinkled face covered with the remains of dinner.

The day passed more quickly than she had thought possible and with it came a rising sense of achievement. It had been so long since she had felt needed – back when her father had been in prison and her mother had leant on her for support. At the end of the day she surprised the staff nurse by telling her she wanted to return.

Over the weeks she worked there, she grew more confident and felt a warm glow every time a face lit up with a smile of recognition when it saw her. She quickly become immune to the ever-present smell and learnt to respect the nurses who worked on the ward. Not only was it back-breaking work but it had its own perils. Toothless old ladies could be underestimated in their agility and age-hardened gums could leave very nasty bruises on a bare wrist that strayed too close.

Soon she knew the names of all the occupants even though most could not remember hers. She helped feed the women, cleaned their faces and changed bedding. As she worked, she smiled at most of the inmates and wagged a finger at others when the bedclothes were stained and the sheets had to be changed.

'Oh, you're being naughty again,' she told them then. She became adept at ducking when an octogenarian threw a tantrum and hurled the nearest missile or spat out a large glop of spittle.

Most importantly, she felt accepted as part of a team.

In the evenings, when she returned wearily to the ward, the card games continued. Her companions thought she was being punished by being sent to work there and Antoinette didn't disillusion them but lapped up the sympathy. After the last hot drink, she would fall into bed, exhausted. Not even the teeth grinding, snores or cries could keep her awake.

Chapter Thirty-Four

Half asleep, Antoinette tentatively explored the inside of her mouth with her tongue. It felt different – something was missing. As her tongue touched her two front teeth, she knew what it was. One of the two crowns she'd had fitted a year earlier had come off. Reaching into her locker, she pulled out a compact and anxiously examined her face. Her reflection confirmed what she had been dreading; instead of the white smile she had taken pride in, there was a filed down stump. She searched the bed in the futile hope that somehow it might have fallen there but when she didn't find it, she guessed with a sinking feeling that she had swallowed it during the night.

Antoinette had seen what happened in those wards when a patient had toothache. The hospital simply arranged for an in-house dentist swiftly to remove the offending tooth. They had found long ago that quick extractions were easier and cheaper than filling the numerous cavities in the teeth of inmates fed on a poor diet. The effort of trying to hold a disturbed patient still for more than a few moments to allow the dentist to explore a cavity was a task none of the staff wanted to undertake. The words 'open wide' and 'it won't hurt' meant little to most of the inmates.

Every morning the trolley arrived with dentures floating in glasses, each one labelled. Before taking the women to the washrooms, the day staff popped ill-fitting false teeth into open mouths. Seeing this morning ritual, Antoinette had asked a nurse why so many women still in their thirties or even younger had dentures. The nurse replied in a matter-of-fact way that the liquid sedatives made the gums recede which weakened the teeth. Plus false teeth were easier to maintain, she said, as they stopped the patients having toothache. She didn't seem to care that this was yet another indignity heaped on the helpless patients.

Antoinette was determined that she was not going to end up with a mouth full of the house-style tombstone dentures and resolved that the hospital dentist with his motto of 'extract, don't fix' was not going anywhere near her mouth. She still had some money saved and she wanted to go to the private dentist who had done her original work. So she asked for a meeting with the ward sister and went to put her case to her.

She had expected numerous obstacles to be put in her path, so she was astonished when the opposite happened.

'Yes, it does need replacing,' agreed the ward sister, looking at the offending stump. 'How much did it cost originally? If you have the money to pay for it, I don't see that there should be any problem. The main difficulty will be that you'll have to be escorted there and back. Leave it with me, Antoinette.'

A few hours later she gave Antoinette the good news. One of the nurses on the dementia ward had agreed to take her to the surgery in her free time.

'I'll phone the dentist myself,' the sister offered, 'then arrange an ambulance to take you.'

She did not know what that act of kindness was going to cost her favourite patient.

The ambulance parked in the street outside the surgery, making it quite clear where this patient had come from. Although the nurse had dressed in 'civvies' to accompany her and Antoinette was not wearing the hospital uniform, the dentist knew well enough who had made the appointment and that this was an inmate of the mental hospital.

'I've brought Antoinette for her appointment,' the nurse announced breezily to the receptionist.

'If you just take a seat I'll let him know you are here.' The receptionist was perfectly polite but Antoinette saw her blanche before she hurried off to inform her boss that his next appointment had arrived. Even though she was dressed in her smartest outfit, Antoinette suddenly knew that the fact she was a patient in a mental hospital had turned her from fee-paying client deserving respect into someone almost frightening. It was obvious that the hospital had not considered her well enough to arrive alone and that the dentist would draw his own conclusions from that. It was not something either she or the ward sister had considered when the appointment was made.

A few minutes later she was ushered in to the surgery. When she had visited the dentist before, he had been full of affable chatter but with her newly acquired status his friendliness had been replaced by a cold, businesslike attitude.

'Open your mouth,' he commanded, and she obeyed. After inspecting her teeth, he said curtly, 'That tooth will have to be drilled. The root has to be removed, and then we can make a post crown.'

Antoinette realized that he wasn't speaking to her – he was addressing all his comments to the nurse. Even though it was her mouth, she didn't seem to exist to him.

Why, she thought. Does he think that being in a mental hospital renders me incapable of hearing or understanding?

The next words filled her with alarm.

'Hold her hands, please, nurse.'

Just as she was wondering why her hands needed holding, she felt a strong grip on her wrists and then, instead of the prick of a needle delivering the painkiller to her gums, she felt her mouth fill with pain. She struggled in her chair, trying to convey the agony she was feeling, so that surely he would stop. She could not believe that he would cause such torment on purpose. Inadvertently, her nails scratched the dentist's hand.

'Hold her tighter,' he snapped, and she felt his anger and impatience at having to treat her.

When the nurse finally released her, she was still shaking with pain. She couldn't believe he had done such a thing to her, or that she had managed to get through it. She found out later that he had removed the nerve from her tooth and not deemed it necessary to inject analgesic into a mental hospital patient.

As the pain subsided, something that felt somehow worse filled her instead. It was the complete humiliation of being treated as something with no feelings. She dug her fingers into her palms to stop herself crying as she listened to him talk to the nurse and make another appointment for the crown to be fitted.

She left the surgery on legs that still shook and jumped thankfully back into the ambulance. All she wanted to do was reach the safety of her ward. She leant her head against the back of her seat and closed her eyes.

Back in the familiar surroundings of the ward, she gave the excuse for not talking that her mouth hurt. She could not bring herself to repeat the details of her treatment. All of a sudden, her perception of the hospital changed. It was where the outside was locked out as opposed to the patients being locked in. Now she saw it as a safe place where she felt accepted and even cared for.

Why would she ever want to leave when the world outside was so harsh?

Chapter Thirty-Five

The first time she met the psychiatrist for her weekly sessions, Antoinette had viewed him with suspicion. Her defences were firmly in place, for she expected him to be another authoritative male who would try and force his interpretation of her childhood on to her. Instead she had found a casually dressed man in his late thirties whose warm smile instantly allayed her fears. He asked her questions, then – unlike the senior doctors she had met in the psychiatric ward – he sat back and waited for her answers.

This doctor made it clear that she did not have to give him details of her past – those he could imagine for himself, he told her. What he wanted instead was to understand the effect it had had on her and what had led up to her being so ill. He asked her to tell him what help she needed to prepare for the future. He further reassured her that if at any time she felt uncomfortable, she could tell him. That was the strategy he wanted to take with her, he had said. Then he put her even more at ease by asking if she was happy with his assessment of her counselling plan. By showing he respected her and what she wanted, he won Antoinette over completely.

In her sessions with him, true to his word, he never once asked her about the reason she had been transferred and never asked one intrusive question about the abuse. Instead, the psychiatrist questioned her about the time she had been at college and seemed more interested in her achievements at school than in her abuse.

He brought up the subject of her work in the hospital and asked if she wanted to work with the mentally ill. 'Sister has told me that you are very good with the old people on the dementia ward. You could get training for that if it is something that interests you.'

'I like them so it's not really difficult. Anyway, it gets me out of the ward and gives me something to do.' She thought for a moment. 'No. That's not really what I want. Anyway –' she grinned '– I would end up not knowing which people were the patients and which ones weren't.'

Like the nurses, he was trying to lead her into a conversation where she might tell him what she really wanted to do in the future. But the thought of leaving frightened her and she did not feel ready to face it.

That day he told her, 'You are almost better, Antoinette, and we want to find a way of helping you leave here. Think about it and we will talk some more in a few days.'

But, unknown to either doctor or patient, there was very little time left. Events outside their control were conspiring to force her to make the decision of whether she wanted to spend her life behind the high brick walls of the hospital or face the outside world again.

The first sign of any change in her routine was a week later, when the ward sister sent for her at a time she was due to go to work. When Antoinette entered the office, the sister closed the door firmly behind her.

'You're not going to the dementia unit today,' she began. 'Your doctor wants to see you. He has something important to discuss with you.' She paused, then leant across the desk to emphasize the importance of her next words. 'Antoinette, do you remember what I said to you when you first came to this ward?'

'Yes. You told me that there are many sad stories in here.'

'And what else did I tell you?' Then, not waiting for her answer, she replied for her. 'That you could be one of my success stories. I want you to remember that when you go to see the doctor.'

A few minutes later Antoinette was sitting in the psychiatrist's office, looking at him aghast. He had dropped his bombshell.

'Your parents are having you sectioned on Tuesday,' he told her calmly. 'That's four days from now.'

He told her that he had discussed the situation with the ward sister before giving her this advance warning. His career could be on the line if it came to the attention of the hospital authorities that a patient had been informed of a decision taken both by senior administrators and the parents of a minor but he thought that Antoinette was worth it.

'You have to understand what your future could be if you allow this to happen. At the moment you have people on your side who have protected you to a certain extent from the reality of life in a long-term ward. Sister has tried to help you in every way she could. But should you be sent to another ward or placed under a different psychiatrist, one of the old school, that protection would end. As a sectioned patient, you would be at risk of electric shock treatment and drugs like Paraldehyde. That's the way patients are kept under control here. It's still on your file that you attacked a patient without provocation. Even if you never give them an excuse to administer electric shock or to be sedated, if you spend another few months here you will become completely institutionalized and incapable of returning to life on the outside.'

He smiled at her then and said what no one in the hospital had expressed before. 'There's nothing wrong with you. You are just a normal person who has reacted to an abnormal situation. You've been put into hospital twice for depression, but you were simply very unhappy. You have been the victim of events you had no control over. You felt rejected – of course you did. You *were* rejected, by your family, by your school, your school friends, even the people who employed you. Your feelings are perfectly natural after what you've gone through. The anger that you felt was a sign that you were recovering. You should feel angry at the people who treated you like that. Your lack of self worth, caused by your childhood, is something that will improve. It already has. You should respect yourself for what you have achieved, for putting yourself through college, and paying your own fees for your secretarial course.

'As for your paranoia,' he continued, 'that is not a term I would use about what has been wrong with you. You have told me that you feel suspicious of people; I think that is perfectly understandable. You felt people were talking about you and while that is a classic symptom of paranoia, in your case it was true. They were talking.' He leaned forward and said earnestly, 'You are not eighteen yet. You have your whole life ahead of you. Don't waste it by staying here, Antoinette. One of the reasons you became ill is that you felt you had no control over your life. Well, you have now. You have to make your mind up to take charge of your future and I know you can do it.'

Then he informed Antoinette of her rights, which up until then she had not understood. 'Don't you know that you are still a voluntary patient? That means you have the right to sign yourself out. Your parents were informed of your transfer from the psychiatric unit to here but it's only now that they have found the time to agree to come to the hospital to sign the consent forms. You are still free to leave. Tomorrow I will be the senior doctor on duty and that means that if you choose to sign yourself out, it is me that you will come to.'

Antoinette experienced a flood of different emotions as he spoke. There was shock at the fact that her parents had known about her transfer, followed by horror that they were prepared to sign forms to commit her. Then confusion and bewilderment at the decision she had to make.

'I wish I didn't have to hurry you into this, or to break the news to you in this manner,' said the doctor. 'But time is short. I want to convince you that your future lies outside these hospital walls. I want you to sit somewhere quiet and think about what I have told you. Your future is in your hands. Sister is going to make you some tea and sandwiches and put you in the visitors' lounge. Take as long as you need and when you have thought it through, I hope you will tell her that you are exercising your rights to leave. If you do that tomorrow morning, she will bring you to me and the one other doctor who has to be present. You must inform us that you are exercising your right as a voluntary patient to sign yourself out.

'Antoinette, I know that you will make the right decision. Once you leave here, never underestimate yourself again. You've survived your childhood, and you have survived being here. That alone is an experience that most people could never have handled.'

Giving her one more encouraging smile, he sent for the sister, who led Antoinette from his office into the visitors' lounge, a room rarely used, with comfortable seating, where she would be undisturbed. The sister brought in tea and biscuits, smiled and then lightly squeezed Antoinette's shoulder as she repeated the words of the doctor.

'I know you will reach the right decision, dear, the one we all want for you.' Then she left, giving Antoinette the time alone to digest the psychiatrist's words.

She understood very clearly that what ever decision she came to over the next few hours would decide the course of her life.

Chapter Thirty-Six

Antoinette knew that loneliness and despair had brought her into the hospital twice. Over the time she had spent in both wards she had come to feel both protected and safe and as she did so the tangle in her head had become gradually unknotted.

She had not ventured outside the confines of the hospital, except for the fateful visit and the equally unpleasant follow-up visit to the dentist, for several months. She had received no visitors since her transfer and had lost touch with the few people she had tentative friendships with. Her mother had not been to visit her once.

It seemed that the more her world had shrunk to the walls of the hospital, the safer she felt. Here she had carved out some semblance of a life, one where she was never lonely. She had a routine, friendships with the nurses and constant company. For the first time since she was fourteen she felt accepted by people who knew her past, something that she doubted she would ever find in the outside world.

She thought of the conversation she had just had with the doctor. There was something niggling her at the back of her mind that she wanted to find and examine. She replayed his words in her memory and as their meaning sunk in, a realization of what the doctor had been trying to tell her hit her like a thunder bolt.

He had said she was a voluntary patient.

A voluntary patient in a psychiatric ward would never have been transferred to the main hospital without the consent of her guardians. The doctor had made it clear that her parents had been notified of her move. They must have told the hospital that they were prepared to commit her then.

No sooner had she grasped that, then other questions crowded her mind, and the answers followed quickly.

Who opened all the post at her parents' house? It was not her father, who was practically illiterate. No, her mother did.

And who answered all the telephone calls? Her mother. Her father disliked it with a passion and always ignored its intrusive ring.

So whom would the hospital have spoken to on the day the psychiatric ward had decided she was too ill to remain there? Her mother.

'You must face it and face it now,' she told herself sternly. 'It was not only your father who wanted rid of you.'

This, Antoinette realized, was the truth and it was something she had run from all her life – that her mother's love for her was worth nothing. It was eleven years since she had felt any affection towards her father, for she had long ago accepted that he was a man who was twisted and warped. With that acceptance she had ceased to question why or make any excuses for him. The months in the hospital had shown her that there were people without any rational explanation for their behaviour; it was just the way they were.

But she had hoped against hope that her mother loved her despite the way she had treated her, and she had wilfully closed her eyes to the real state of affairs and the harsh reality of her mother's actions. But she could do so no longer. Now she had to confront the weakness and shallowness of her mother's love for her. And she had to know that it was this that had almost destroyed her for a second time.

In her early childhood it was her mother who had been the centre of Antoinette's life. She was the person who picked her up when she fell and dried her eyes when she cried. At night it was her mother who bathed her, rinsed soapy water from her small face then carried her, wrapped in a fluffy towel, to the bedroom to be rubbed dry and sprinkled with talcum powder. Ruth had tucked her into bed and read her a story before dimming the light and kissing her goodnight. She could remember her mother sitting in a chair with a lamp on the small table beside her, its glow illuminating her lowered head as she patiently put the last touches to the latest dress she had made for her daughter.

Her mother's familiar perfume of face powder mixed with the lingering scent of jasmine had comforted her, as did the warmth of her body when she was cuddled by her. It was her arms that had held the young Antoinette close, her heart that beat against her small daughter's chest and her voice that told the little girl about fairies and magic when she read bedtime stories out loud. And it was Ruth's hand that held her smaller one tightly when they crossed a road – 'to keep you safe,' she had said.

That was the mother she had always loved. That was the mother she had always refused to accept no longer existed. But the truth was that she had stopped being that mother when Antoinette was six.

It was then that coldness had replaced the warmth, the goodnight kisses stopped and protective arms had ceased to cuddle her. Ruth had stopped all that from the day that Antoinette had told her what her father did to her.

Before now, when the memory of that day threatened to penetrate her mind, she had pushed it aside. Now she wanted to examine it.

She summoned up the picture of her six-year-old self gathering up the courage to tell her mother that her father had touched and kissed her. Back then, the little girl had thought that by telling, it would be stopped. She remembered the expressions that had flitted across Ruth's face that day: the love had vanished and it was replaced by anger and fear. But, Antoinette realized now, Ruth's face had registered neither surprise nor shock.

'I understand now,' she murmured. 'I'm beginning to see how it was.'

Now that her memories had forced themselves into her mind, she did not push them away. This time she knew that she had to deal with them because she had to examine her mother's role in her life.

Who was her mother? She remembered the caring mother of her early childhood, the one she had adored. Then she recalled the cold, remote Ruth of the years of the abuse until the end of the court case. She had feared that mother. Then there was the laughing, chatting friend from the two years they spent together at the gate lodge. Finally there was the mother who had betrayed her trust, the one who had taken her husband back, thrown her daughter out and committed her to hospital.

A memory rose to the surface of her mind. When she had come to hospital months before in a state of such

depression and isolation she could not speak, she had experienced a brief spell of coherence. She had telephoned her
mother, pleading with her to visit. Ruth had berated her
daughter for her selfishness and down the line Antoinette had
heard the refrain that had been repeated so often over the
years. She was a constant source of worry, and that worry was
enough to drive Ruth into the same place her daughter was.

'It should be me in there instead of you,' were her final
words before the phone went dead.

'What kind of mother says that? What mother doesn't visit
her daughter in hospital even once?' Antoinette asked herself.
And what kind of daughter continues to fool herself that her
mother is hiding her love for her? Who carries on believing
in a person who ceased to exist years before?

Antoinette had come to learn that memories are treacherous things and as she sat in the lounge, she faced another
painful truth. Memories had invented a loving mother and a
perfect love that had never existed, and Antoinette had never
stopped believing those false memories. When it became too
difficult to sustain the illusion any longer, Antoinette had
blamed herself for what she had understood as a sudden with-
drawal of maternal affection. She must be weak and bad and
worthless. The key to the loss of her mother's love must lie
within herself.

She had so often opened the box stored inside her mind and
taken out those memories of her mother protecting, cherish-
ing and playing with her. The other times when Ruth had
done none of those things Antoinette had completely obliterated from her mind. She realized now that her mother had
always managed to turn things round and convince her that
her, Ruth's, version of reality was the true one. Ruth had
turned innocence into guilt, and the victim into the wrong-

doer and she had forced Antoinette to accept that was how it was. She had made Antoinette her accomplice in rewriting the truth.

Sitting in the quiet visitors' lounge, Antoinette tried to put everything she had learned about her mother over the years into some semblance of order. If she could understand why Ruth had become such a bitter discontented woman, maybe it would help her come to terms with her mother's actions.

What lay behind the mask and lived in the mind of a woman with those different faces?

That was the question she wanted to answer before she spoke to either the sister or the psychiatrist and she knew that somewhere buried in her memories lay the clues that could lead her to an understanding.

Chapter Thirty-Seven

During the long evenings at the gate lodge, Ruth had often told stories of her own childhood.

The elder of two children, Ruth had been christened Winifred Ruth Rowden – 'an ugly name' she said often, with the pained expression of one who knows she has been badly treated. Ruth remembered her childhood as an unhappy one. Her mother Isabelle was a beautiful petite woman whom Antoinette had loved as a grandmother but whom she knew her mother found difficult. Even as a small girl, she could sense the discord between the two.

'She was always so proud of her figure,' Ruth had often said in withering tones.

Ruth's father had been a dark, handsome man whom she had clearly idolized and it seemed to Antoinette that her mother had resented her parents' happy marriage. 'He was always under her thumb, of course,' she said with disdain when she talked about them. Then, with a humourless laugh, she would say, 'Somehow she had him convinced that she was delicate and needed looking after but you know, dear, what a will of iron your grandmother really has. Your uncle, of course, was the apple of her eye. Whereas I was my father's favourite. To him, I was beautiful.'

Once Antoinette had told her mother that she wished for a baby brother and Ruth had said that she had never wanted hers. It seemed she had decided as child that younger brothers served no useful purpose and even as an adult, she had not changed her mind. She had never forgiven him for stealing her parents' attention away from her and, later in life, his successful marriage and happiness constantly rankled. No wonder she had decided not to inflict the same fate on her own daughter.

There was a family photograph that showed Antoinette's grandparents, her mother and her uncle in a stiff formal portrait taken in the early years of the twentieth century. It showed a handsome boy of about seven years old and a girl around ten sitting by the feet of two good-looking adults. The young Ruth looked a morose, sullen child, inclined to overindulge in eating. Nevertheless, Ruth's reminiscences of her early childhood painted a picture of a happy time, before the First World War.

Her adored father had been a master tailor in Golders Green and it was a great treat for Ruth to be taken to the workshops. There, she would watch the men he employed as they sat cross-legged on the floor, painstakingly stitching the cut cloth and turning it into garments. The little girl felt so special when she was there – she was the treasured daughter of the boss, the little pet of all the men there. They gave her material, showed her how to stitch and it was there that she learnt her skill in dressmaking. She much preferred to be the centre of attention among the tailors than to be at home, with a mother she disliked and a brother she resented.

Then, when Ruth was twenty, her father died suddenly. She was grief stricken. Her father had only been in his early fifties and his death was utterly unexpected.

'It was a blood clot that moved to his brain,' Ruth told her daughter sadly every time she spoke of the man who had been the most important person in her life. 'He worked too hard. He was always trying to please *her*,' she said bitterly.

Antoinette knew that Ruth meant her mother, Isabelle, and that in some way, she blamed her for her father's death.

The household was left completely bereft without its master. Now Ruth's brother, three years younger and blessed with good looks, a gentle disposition and his mother's love, was the man of the house. Ruth, still living at home as was usual at the time, found herself outnumbered.

'My brother adored our mother, just like every other man,' she would say with badly concealed resentment. 'Well, he went and married a woman just like her.'

Later, when her mother talked about her brother's wife, Antoinette sensed an aversion towards her and had not understood it. She only remembered a very pretty woman who had always made her welcome when she and Ruth had made one of their infrequent visits to her uncle's London flat.

The Second World War had begun, bringing with it speedy romances and fast marriages. Within eighteen months of war being declared, Ruth's brother had got married and produced a child. Meanwhile, Ruth, three years older, was still a spinster – 'another ugly name,' she sniffed to Antoinette. She minded that she was still unmarried and was jealous that her brother had found what she wanted – a spouse. To be almost thirty and still single was not to be envied at a time when women were judged by the status of the man they married.

But the war brought excitement, adventure and opportunity into Ruth's life and she often said later that her experiences then were some of the happiest she had ever known. She did her bit for the war effort by working on a farm. It was there, out of the shadow of her mother and brother, that Ruth had blossomed and made friends. She was conscious of her age, though, and of the fact that she had no boyfriend in her life to swap gossip about. To protect herself from the pity of the other girls, she invented one and told her new friends that he had been her fiancé, but that he had been killed in the first week of the war. By the time she told Antoinette the story ten years later, she had come to believe it herself.

It was Ruth's mother Isabelle who told Antoinette that it was a wild exaggeration. The 'fiancé' had been a married soldier who had once shared tea and scones with Ruth in a corner café. 'I worry about her sometimes, Antoinette,' her grandmother had confided to her. 'She makes things up and then she starts believing them.'

During the war, Ruth met her future husband. She had gone to a local dance in Kent with a group of women from the farm where she worked. That night, she wore a becoming dress with a short bolero jacket that she had designed and stitched herself. Her girlfriends thought it was wonderful and were all the more impressed that she had made it herself.

On that hot noisy evening at the end of June, the women's interest was attracted by a crowd of young servicemen who were dressed in well-pressed khaki uniforms and looked far more dashing then the men they were used to. The girls sat nearby and threw surreptitious glances at the young soldiers. One in particular caught their attention. He had twinkling eyes, a wide ready smile, and his dark auburn waves gleamed as brightly as his well-polished boots. Not only that but he showed a talent for dancing they'd never seen before as he waltzed a girl around the room.

His name was Joe Maguire and all the girls would have given plenty to be held in his arms with their feet dancing on air. Suddenly he appeared at Ruth's side.

'Dance?' was the first word she heard him say.

'Of course!' she shouted inwardly, almost overcome that he had approached her and not one of the younger women, but she kept her outward composure, gave him a sweet smile and followed him to the dance floor.

That was the night he entered her life. After that first magical dance, he claimed every one as his. The handsome young serviceman literally swept her off her feet and found his way into her heart. She saw the looks of jealousy that appeared on other women's faces and relished being the envy of her friends.

Ruth did not see the five-year age difference, hear the thickness of his Irish accent or notice his lack of education; she was completely mesmerized by his good looks and fell under the spell of his charm. That was the night the twenty-nine-year-old spinster found her hero. And Joe Maguire, a man who craved respect and recognition, saw a woman with poise who spoke in an upper-class accent, the sort he had never imagined having the good fortune to meet.

A few weeks later, on the thirteenth of August, they married. For different reasons neither of them quite believed their luck. She was thankful that he had rescued her from the disgrace of still being single at thirty and he believed he had found the woman who would win him the admiration he craved in his home town.

If it had not been for the war those two unsuited people would never have met. But Ruth felt she had achieved the first part of her dream: a handsome husband. Thirteen months later, their daughter was born.

* * *

As Antoinette pondered what she knew of her mother, she realized that the jigsaw was not yet complete. There was still something missing and Antoinette searched deeper into her mind to find it. She finally extracted two more memories and with them the explanation of the enigma that was her mother fell into place.

She saw herself in a tea shop. Dressed in her best frock, which her mother had finished making that week, she sat contentedly on a cushion that had been placed on a chair. Her discreetly made-up grandmother was wearing a light suit and a matching cloche hat from which curling tendrils of red gold hair escaped. She was treating Antoinette and her mother to afternoon tea.

Ruth was a sharp contrast to Isabelle, with her scarlet nails and matching lipstick. Her permed hair was uncovered and large gold hooped earrings dangled from her ears. That day she was wearing a new square-necked print dress of her own design. Both women looked happy as they chattered together.

Then an elderly woman, who clearly knew her grand-mother, approached their table to be greeted with a welcoming smile from Isabelle. After some pleasantries, the stranger exclaimed, 'Belle, I don't know how you do it, you look younger every time I see you and this pretty little girl's growing to be the spitting image of you. One would almost think she was your daughter, not Ruth's!' And, with a light laugh, she left.

Antoinette felt the warmth that had engulfed the three of them dissipate as though a cold draft had blown into the tea shop. For a few seconds an uneasy silence hung in the air until Ruth broke it with some light-hearted comment told in a brittle voice. Even at five years old, Antoinette knew without understanding why that her mother was displeased at the compliment she had been paid.

The second memory was when she was three years older. She was doing what all little girls take a delight in, dressing up in their mother's clothes, playing with her make-up and pretending to be an adult. She had smudged rouge into her cheeks and painted her mouth a vibrant red as she had seen her mother do so often. Then she hoisted up her over-long dress and went looking for her mother. She wanted to show Ruth how pretty she had made herself. But when she ran up to her with her arms out for a cuddle, she was surprised. Instead of the smile of pleasure she had anticipated, Ruth looked at her frostily.

'Underneath that make up, you look just like your grand-mother,' she said. 'Your eyes could be hers looking at me. Well, you are certainly going to be better looking than your mother.'

Looking back and remembering what she had heard and the tone of her mother's voice, Antoinette knew that her mother had not liked what she had seen. She had never played dressing up again.

Now those incidents came together in Antoinette's head. She understood properly that her mother had been plagued throughout her life by her insecurity and jealousy. Ruth had been jealous of her own mother, jealous of the love her father had felt for his wife, the devotion of her brother to his mother and the fragile beauty of Isabelle herself. That jealousy grew to include anyone who took away the attention that she thought was rightfully hers. And once her daughter had stopped being a malleable baby and had become a small person, her jealousy had extended to her.

And then there was Ruth's need to keep up appearances and her fear of what other people thought of her. Her whole life and all her relationships had been sacrificed to maintain a fiction that she could show to the world and come to believe in herself. She created a tissue of lies, a pretend existence where her handsome husband was a man she was proud of, not an ignorant beast who had subjected their child to abuse.

As she thought back over her life, Antoinette accepted that Ruth's maternal love had been totally eclipsed by her need to protect her dream.

Joe's hold over his wife was a powerful one. He had long ago honed his ability to read those around him, search out their vulnerabilities and then control his victims. His wife, whose mind was forever locked on the handsome Irish man she had married against her family's wishes, was completely under his thumb. He had wanted to control Antoinette too, and once she was a teenager, with a mind of her own, he had set out to break her. When that didn't work, he wanted nothing to do with her. Joe could not stand to have anyone around him who did not think he was wonderful. He had no wish to look into his daughter's eyes and see the contempt there. Even the sound of his daughter's name made him angry.

Ruth had to choose. And she chose him, every time. She had watched his cruelty and allowed it. She chose him even when she knew that he had made their daughter pregnant, and when she arranged for Antoinette to have an abortion. That abortion had gone horribly wrong and on the night that Antoinette had woken, in danger of haemorrhaging to death, Ruth had even been willing to risk sacrificing her daughter's life, sending her alone in the ambulance to a hospital thirteen miles away from the nearest one. She had refused to accompany her daughter on that journey, a journey that she must have known could have been the final one. Antoinette remembered the shock on the ambulance driver's face as they picked up the stretcher and her mother's cold stare as the doors closed with her remaining outside, and the ambulance with blue lights flashing began its race against time.

Ruth must have been told that, after that, Antoinette would never be able to have children. She had never said a word.

And then there was the breakdown that had brought her to this place. What had brought it to pass? What had finally made Antoinette collapse completely?

She had learnt coping strategies early. By the age of ten, she had created a room in her mind where she could retreat when the reality of her existence became too much to bear. Only in her imaginary world could she pretend to be what she thought a normal child was. In this room she was beautifully dressed, always surrounded by chattering little girls who vied for her attention and wanted to be her best friend. Here she was popular, listened to and the room rang with laughter. The sun always shone when she retreated there, its rays filtering through unseen windows bathed her in their warm golden light.

Her parents would visit, their faces wreathed in smiles as they hugged her, making her feel special. It was always the nice father who arrived with her mother, the man she remembered him being when she was five years old; of the nasty one there was no sign. In that room her mother was happy without the lines of discontent that ran down her face. Judy still remained a mischievous puppy who played on the floor, while in the corner stood her memory boxes. The one with bad memories was tightly sealed, the contents forbidden to escape, while the smaller box containing the good ones stood open.

But then, as Antoinette grew older, the room became a dark place, empty of friends where only her mother came. But this was not the mother of her childhood dreams, the mother who loved and cuddled her. This mother looked at her with coldness while her dark green eyes both accused and reproached her. In the corners of the room the boxes had been reversed. It was the lid of the larger one containing the bad memories that had sprung open, spewing out its contents with no thought of order, creating a malevolent sprit that invaded her dreams and whispered to her she was to blame, not the people who rejected her. That spirit tormented her nightly until her mind was in complete chaos.

Then, when she had fallen ill and her mother had sent her away, the cataclysmic nature of Ruth's betrayal became clear. It was then that she finally lost her fight to be a normal teenager. Inside our heads there is a space which is completely blank. It holds no memories and has no thoughts. Antoinette wanted to find that place for once there, the world no longer has the power to hurt. She wanted to curl up in the cocoon of her bedding until that time came and never have to face reality again.

It was then that her mind had buckled under the onslaught and she had ended up in hospital.

Antoinette thought sadly again of the facts that she had pieced together. First, that as a voluntary patient she could never have been transferred without her mother's permission. Second, that Ruth had never made any effort to visit her daughter and see for herself if any progress had been made. And third, that Ruth had always known what her husband was.

She got up from her seat and pressed the buzzer on the wall. She was ready now.

A few minutes later the ward sister entered and sat opposite her patient. 'Well, have you decided what you're going to do tomorrow?' she asked.

Instead of answering her question Antoinette looked at her squarely in the face and said, 'Do you know how the dictionary defines incest? I looked it up once.'

'No. Tell me.'

'The sexual union between persons who are so closely related that their marriages are illegal or contrary to custom. Or their copulation is illegal. The people who commit it are considered impure. But that's not what it is.'

'Tell me what it is.'

'It is rape, it is a thousand rapes.' It was the first time Antoinette had voiced those thoughts to anyone. She looked at the bars on the windows, and realized that a year after her father's release, she was still in her prison of memories. She continued in a voice more resigned than sad. 'My mother took back a man who had raped me one thousand times. That's how many three times a week for seven years is. His prison sentence was less than one day for each time he did that. One thousand times – and then it was me she told to leave.'

The ward sister sat silently, as though she knew how much it must have cost the seventeen-year-old to come to terms with the facts of her life.

For a moment Antoinette wavered, and then in her mind's eye she saw the rows of cots with the white-haired old ladies. She heard the cries and moans from the women waking from their electric-shock sessions and saw their glazed unfocused eyes as they looked around helplessly, the remnants of their memory slipping further away with each treatment.

Then she thought of her mother and how she had wasted her life on broken promises and unfulfilled dreams and nearly destroyed her daughter as she did so.

Antoinette knew that if she stayed inside the walls of the hospital, then, like her mother, she could escape from the truths of her life that hurt her. But by doing so, she would throw away her future.

She remembered suddenly the day she fell from her cousin Hazel's horse. Hazel had said, 'You have to get back on the horse. If you don't, you never will, you'll always be afraid.' She had summoned up her courage and obeyed her cousin. Antoinette knew that this was the time to do it again.

'I'm going to sign myself out,' she said simply.

The following morning she wrote her name on the release forms with a flourish: Toni Maguire.

It was Toni who left the hospital. Antoinette the frightened teenager was no longer there.

Chapter Thirty-Eight

The night before I left hospital, I made my mind up that the games my mother had played had come to the end. I was never again going to be party to her psychological manipulation.

Instead I telephoned her. 'I'm better,' I said briefly. 'I've made a full recovery. The hospital has told me I'm well enough to leave. And I'm coming to see you for a visit.'

I knew my mother; she would not fight the opinion of the doctors and the medical establishment. And I was right. She was so taken aback by my lack of submission that she put up no resistance.

As I turned into their road that day, I saw that my mother's dream of owning her own large house had finally come true during the time I had been in hospital. A few months before my release they had moved and the doctor had furnished me with their new address. The house was a white double-storied building standing back from the road, in a smart suburb of Belfast.

They sold the gate lodge for a good profit, I thought. I stood for a few seconds looking at the exterior of what should have been a happy family home. But I knew the truth. My parents would grow old together with only their terrible secret to keep them company.

My mother flung open the door as soon as I had knocked. As soon as I looked at her, I knew everything had changed. Where was the mother I remembered, the one who could intimidate me with a glance one moment and then release boundless affection the next? This woman looked smaller, diminished somehow and I realized for the first time that I was the taller by several inches. An air of defeat had settled heavily about her, her shoulders drooped and her eyes slid away from mine as though to hide her emotions.

Did she remember the times she had betrayed my trust, I wondered. Or has she even rewritten that part of our family history?

She stood aside to allow me to enter, then she made us both tea. Once it was poured, she asked me what my plans were.

'I want to go to England,' I replied and felt sadness at the look of relief that appeared on her face even though I'd expected it.

'When did you have in mind, darling?'

'As soon as possible. There's an agency here that can find me hotel work. I want to be a receptionist. That will provide me with accommodation as well as a good wage.'

I did not ask my mother if I could stay with her but simply took my case to a bedroom and she did not protest. I stayed there for three days before leaving for England.

I managed to avoid seeing my father almost entirely. He was keen to keep out of the way and barely came home while I was there. He did not say goodbye when I left.

I hugged my mother when I said goodbye, promised to write to her and then jumped in the taxi that took me to the docks.

I never told my parents that I knew they had been going to commit me. Confrontation would have gained nothing and

I had already made my plans. I had erected a barrier against the old love I had felt for my mother as soon as the teenager I had been disappeared.

As I stood on the deck and watch the gangway being hauled up and Belfast disappear from view, I knew that I would never return – not to live, anyway. And as for the promises of letters … well, that was a promise I had every intention of breaking.

When the last light of the city had vanished, I went to the bar, ordered a glass of wine and toasted myself.

To a new life.

Chapter Thirty-Nine

I pulled my mind back from the past and tried to push away the memories of Antoinette, and the child she had been over thirty years ago. I poured myself a stiff drink, lit a cigarette and reflected instead on the person I had become.

Antoinette had entered that hospital but it was Toni who had finally faced her parents before leaving Ireland. Without words, she had shown them that her past was put to rest where theirs never would be.

Two years later my mother traced and then contacted me. It only took one tearful phone call for us to resume the game of happy families. Later, I discovered that during my time in hospital, the hospital had repeatedly asked Ruth to visit me. They had said that without her, there was little chance of her daughter recovering – this was more than a bout of depression or a nervous breakdown and they were not confident that I would be able to cope in the outside world again. The doctors had made clear to Ruth what the problem was:

'Your daughter simply cannot come to terms with the fact that you knew what was happening to her for all those years,' they said.

Ruth had not reacted well to this. It struck at the heart of everything she had pretended to herself. But she still refused to accept for a moment that she might be in some way to blame. 'Doctor, how dare you accuse me? I did not know. I've suffered enough. I've never received any sympathy, only Antoinette has. It should be me in there, not her. If she needs to see a parent so badly I'll send her father. She should be his responsibility.'

That was the last time the hospital contacted my mother. But still, knowing even this, I could not find it within myself to reject her completely.

Over the next thirty years, I did many things. I owned my own businesses, crossed Kenya by bus and successfully sued a greedy business partner in the high court. I became a woman comfortable in her own skin, one who had learnt to rely on the friendship of others and to like herself, and who had learnt how to be happy. But I never had the courage to break contact with my parents.

Oh, in later years my mother grew to love me. I was Toni, the successful daughter, who would arrive in Ireland on holiday with an armful of presents, take her out and never mention my past. I allowed my mother to fit me back into the dream she had created: a good-looking husband, her own house and one daughter.

As the adult, I knew that it was many years too late to challenge my mother's fantasy life. To take it away would have destroyed her.

But she did not manage to leave this life without facing the truth again. During her last days in the hospice, where I came to sit with her and hold her hand until the end, my mother became frightened. She was not frightened of dying but of meeting the God she believed in. Did she think her sins were beyond forgiveness? Perhaps. Whatever the reason, she fought death while wishing for it.

From her doctor, nurse and minister, I knew enough of my mother's time in the hospice before I arrived to be able to picture her torment as clearly as if I had been there. I could imagine it vividly:

An old woman stirred in her sleep as she lay in her bed on the ward. Pain penetrated her consciousness, forcing her awake. She tried to keep her eyes shut, for terror held her firmly in its grip. An image floated behind her closed eyelids: a small bedroom lit only by the yellow glow thrown by a single unshaded bulb and the ambulance's flashing blue light. A frightened teenager lay on the bed, the bottom half of her thin cotton pyjamas soaked with blood and her eyes pleading for help.

She forced that picture away only for it only to be replaced by another; one that she wanted to make disappear but try as she might, she could not make it go. This time it was of a psychiatrist, accusing her of trying to send a child to her death.

That simply was not true, she protested. She had sent her daughter to the better hospital, everyone knew it was the place Antoinette ought to go ...

Full of panic, she pressed the emergency button that lay on her bed and lay back panting to wait for the nurse.

'Ruth,' she heard the gentle voice say, 'what's wrong?'

With her genteel English accent my mother replied, 'I need to see the minister, I need to talk to him tonight.'

'Can it not wait until morning? He's only just gone and sure, the poor man's been here over twelve hours and he did come to you last night, don't you remember?

The old lady was impervious to the plea. 'No, dear, I might be dead by the morning.' Here the voice sweetened and her fingers, still surprisingly strong, clasped the nurse's hand. The dark green eyes closed briefly hiding the steely determination that lived in their depths. 'I need him now.'

'All right, Ruth, if it's that important to you, I'll ring him.' With that, the nurse drifted quietly away on her crepe-soled shoes.

The old woman lay back on her pillows with a sigh of contentment and a half smile on her lips. Even in here, she intended getting her own way.

Minutes passed, then she heard the heavier tread of the minister. He drew up a chair and felt his hand touch hers.

'Ruth,' she heard him say. 'Tell me what I can do for you.'

She groaned as another wave of pain gripped her and looked at him with an expression that suddenly made him feel uneasy. 'My daughter. I want her to come.'

'Why, Ruth, I didn't know you had a daughter!' he exclaimed with surprise.

'Oh yes, but we don't see her very often, she lives in London. But she phones every week to see how I am and I always make her speak to her father. She's doing all right for herself. She'll come if her father tells her to. I'll speak to him tomorrow.'

The minister wondered briefly why again he had been called out in the middle of the night but decided to let her talk, hoping this time she would open up to him.

Her fingers gripped his tighter. 'I have terrible dreams,' she finally admitted.

Looking into her eyes, he saw the fear there and knew there was more than her illness causing it. 'Ruth, is something troubling you? Is there something you want to tell me? Is there something you think I should know?'

The old woman hesitated, but eventually whispered, 'No, I'll be all right when my daughter comes.'

And with that she turned away and fell into a restless sleep. The minister left, feeling that he was leaving a troubled soul whom he had failed to help for the second time in twenty-four hours.

After my mother's request, my father phoned me.

It was that telephone call that took me to her side. The fact that she needed me was all the motivation I had needed to make that journey.

I spent long days and nights at her side as she slowly slipped closer to death. While I was there, I felt the presence of the ghost of my childhood. The Antoinette I had once been came back to me and made me look at how things had really been. She unpicked strand by strand the fabric of the lies I had told myself.

'My mother loved me,' I had protested.

'She loved him more,' she had retorted. 'She committed the ultimate betrayal. Let your love for her go.'

But I could not obey her. I was still unwilling to face up to my mother's treachery. I felt again the wave of love mixed with pity that had been the mixture of emotions that my mother had roused in me for so many years. She had remained loyal to the man who had abused their daughter and there was no justification for the part she played but I had always made excuses for her in the past.

Now I had to accept, finally, the reality of my own definition of my parents. There was one who was the perpetrator but there was also one who was guilty of passively watching but doing nothing, absolutely nothing, to stop years of abuse.

There, as I sat at her side in my vigil, I accepted the enormity of what she had done and was overwhelmed with a terrible sadness. I grieved for the woman I had always believed she could have been; I grieved for the happy, loving relationship we could have had and, during her final days, I mourned the fact that it was far too late for us now. And I accepted that, try as I had over the years, I had never stopped loving her. Even when I had come to accept that a woman who does nothing to protect her child from a terrible crime is as guilty as the perpetrator, I could not change my feelings. Love, as I have found, is a hard habit to break.

My mother was dead and now I was burying my father. I thought again of Antoinette, the child she had been, how she loved her animals and her books, how much she was capable of. She had survived her time in the institution. She had made friends and emerged stronger and more independent than before. It so easily could have been different. But it wasn't.

I thought of what she had achieved and, for the first time, I felt something other than the sadness her name had always evoked.

I felt pride. Pride in what she had accomplished.

'Don't let her down,' I said to myself firmly. 'Don't let her struggle and her survival be in vain. Unless you allow the two halves of yourself that you keep separate to meet and join, you will never be a whole person. Your parents are dead now. Let them go.'

I looked into the mirror, almost expecting to see the teenage Antoinette looking back at me but the reflection showed very little of the child I had once been. Instead I saw a middle-aged woman whose blonde-streaked hair framed a face that was carefully made up; a woman whose appearance was important to her.

Then the face softened and smiled back and, as it did so, I saw a woman who had finally let her demons go.

There was only one thing left for me to do in Larne and once done, I would have finished with the past. Tomorrow I had to face the relatives that I had not seen for thirty years and mingle with the local townspeople who had liked and admired my father. Then I would be free at last.

Chapter Forty

The sun shone on the day of my father's funeral.

My friend's phone had been constantly ringing with calls from the local town people with sincere commiserations and my friends in England with quite different comments. One had arranged to fly over to give me support and I was relieved that there would be someone there who would understand how I felt.

My uncle, whom I had not seen since I was fourteen, was due to make an appearance along with his sons. I had rung them the day after his death and spoken to my uncle for the first time in over thirty years.

It was obvious that this was the funeral of a popular man – 'Good old Joe', a man still possessed of good looks and charm right up into his eighties; a man whom the town would turn out in droves for; a man they wanted to honour as they paid their last respects.

Joe's photograph had appeared in local newspapers alongside an article praising his triumph at yet another amateur golf tournament and his legendary skill with the snooker cue. My father's unpredictable temper, which had been shown in flashes when he had lost a game of snooker, missed a stroke at golf or received some imagined slight, was to be forgotten.

It was Joe Maguire, with his infectious smile and silver-tongued charm, that they would all remember.

How did his younger brother recall him, I wondered. What stories had he told his sons – my father's nephews and my cousins?

I dressed carefully, not as a sign of respect for him but as protective armour for me. A black suit was donned, matching shoes and bag had been chosen, make-up carefully applied and my now blonde highlighted hair washed and blow dried. Would they recognize me? After all, there was little sign of Antoinette, the child who had once been me.

No longer did she haunt me; no longer did I see her face, feel her fears and share her nightmares. It was three years since I had looked in the mirror and seen her eyes looking back at me. But I knew that deep in my mind in that corner we keep hidden even from ourselves, she was still there and had never left. That day I sensed her presence beside me. I felt her desire to be remembered and understood her anger at her inability to hate the man who had destroyed her.

Once, many years ago, my father's relatives had been Antoinette's too, but she had been banished from their hearts when they had chosen to stand by her father. For them I felt nothing. The pain of missing them was healed and the scars left by their rejection were well hidden. Now for the first time since I had been a child I was going to have to confront them.

The mirror showed the reflection of Toni, the successful businesswoman. On her face was a determined expression showing that she was the only person they were going to see.

The minister who was to take the service was the same one who had buried my mother and the one I had talked to when my memories had threatened to overwhelm me three years ago when my mother had died. He had not wanted to take this service, giving the fact that my father had moved outside his parish as an excuse but I had pleaded with him to do so. I knew he recalled those days when I had stayed with my mother at the hospice during her final weeks of her life. I had sat at her bedside when the cancer that she had been fighting for nearly two years finally won. It was there that my father's daily visits had almost shattered the protective barrier I had built against Antoinette, the ghost of my childhood. The minister knew only too well how I had come to him distraught, thinking that I was regressing into that frightened child again. Through me, he knew the man my father had been, the harm he had done, the lives he had destroyed and his lack of remorse.

I needed his presence, I told him. His strength and essential goodness would give me the support I needed to act out the role of dutiful daughter for the last time. He knew without my telling him that with this funeral service I wanted the past buried. And we both recalled my mother's cheerless funeral when my father had refused to invite anyone back to the house after the service and would not allow refreshments to be arranged anywhere else. That day the mourners who had turned out to support me had returned home after the funeral service without even being offered a cup of tea. My father had gone to the pub. It was a bleakness of a farewell unheard of in hospitable Ireland. Not for my isolated mother the offer from the British Legion to host a reception. It was as though the years she had lived in Ireland had never existed.

'Good old Joe' walked away from such an act of disloyalty with his reputation intact. For wasn't he the poor widower who had nursed his wife through years of illness? And hadn't he done that with little help from a daughter seemingly well off? A daughter who seldom left England and had only arrived to help with her mother once she was safely in the hospice?

The town was determined that his funeral would be a very different affair. Some of the town's folk were already gathered outside the funeral parlour when I arrived. Out of respect for the woman they believed to be the chief mourner, they stood aside allowing me to enter first. They would, I knew give me several minutes before they followed, time to say a last farewell and compose myself.

I climbed the steps of the funeral parlour as I had three years ago and entered the small room where its rows of seats had prayer books placed on each chair. I looked at my father lying in his open coffin and felt nothing except a bleak sadness at the end of this era.

He lay as though asleep; thick hair was swept back from a face tinged with colour and his teeth now replaced showed through lips that were creased into a slight smile. Once again his face was handsome, for the mortician had worked with skilful hands. I had a chilling feeling that he was still there, dreaming of happy times with no troubled thoughts to disturb him. Somehow I felt that his spirit still lingered, scorning me for the last time.

The day before I had given the keys of my father's house to one of his friends with the request that he choose appropriate clothes to bury him in. I could not bring myself to go into his bedroom, open his cupboards and touch his belongings. Not before I knew he had finally gone.

His friend had chosen well. My father wore a grey worsted suit complete with freshly laundered handkerchief tucked into breast pocket while an army tie was firmly knotted under the collar of his carefully ironed cream shirt. His medals, won during the war, were proudly displayed as a reminder that he had been one of the brave thousands of Northern Irish men who had volunteered to fight for their country.

In death, 'Good old Joe' was a dignified man, ready to receive his visitors for the last time and I, his daughter, stood at my expected place by his side.

My father's relatives, led in by my uncle. For the first time since I was fourteen we were in the same room. Although my uncle was shorter and slighter than my father, he bore such an uncanny resemblance to him that I found it unnerving. The same luxuriant white hair was swept back from an unreadable face, in the style of his brother and their father before them. He stared into the coffin and whatever emotion he felt as he looked at the brother that once he had admired and loved was hidden.

As he turned to walk away I placed myself firmly in front of him.

'Hello, Uncle,' I said. 'Thank you for coming.' Then I stretched my hand out to receive his.

His eyes refused to meet mine as our hands limply touched in a simulation of a handshake. Still not looking directly at me he muttered, 'Hello.'

Without comment or commiseration he continued walking to the opposite side of the funeral parlour. His son and nephews followed and I knew that nothing had changed.

Had I hoped for a family reconciliation? Maybe in my subconscious I had. Instead I placed a neutral smile on my face and greeted the next mourner who was waiting to come to the coffin. One by one they came, bent over it and looked at my father's face before taking their seats. The room was full of hushed voices and the odd handkerchief could be seen wiping away a tear.

The funeral director, a tall well-built man who had shown kindness when he had arranged my mother's funeral, sensed that something was wrong and went to inform my father's relatives that there were refreshments arranged for after the funeral and he hoped to see them there. Politely but firmly they made their excuses. They had come for one reason only – to see Joe, their brother, uncle, and cousin, buried. His daughter was to remain the outsider.

Separated from them not just by the aisle but by a gulf that the years had not breached, I felt the momentary loss of what could have been. Standing alone, I looked forward at my father's coffin. His face seemed to look up at me and in my imagination his smile now mocked me. I heard the words he had uttered so many times.

'People won't love you, Antoinette, if you tell. Everyone will blame you.'

And there, a few feet away from me, was the family who did.

My friend, seeing I was not going to be joined by my family, came to my side, smiled gently at me to show love and support, and my courage returned. I shut out that voice from the past, stilled the regrets I had not allowed myself to feel for thirty years, and began the process of greeting the rest of the many locals who had turned up to show their respect for my father and their support for me, his daughter.

My attention was caught by a woman who stood alone as though wanting privacy for her thoughts. In her early seventies with short grey blonde hair styled into the nape of her neck and a well-cut dark suit showing off her slim figure, she had an air of elegance about her which made her stand out in the small funeral parlour. She had an upright stance; age had not made her spine hunch with the onset of years. The fine cobweb of lines on her face on another day I knew would reflect humour and character but now only sadness showed as her gaze lingered on the coffin.

Her grief touched me but when she caught my eye I saw apprehension mix with her sorrow. I smiled as reassuringly as I could and she summoned up her courage to approach. I touched her hand briefly for I knew that speech had temporarily deserted her. She, thinking I was distressed as well, quietly sat nearby and picked up a prayer book.

Words could wait until later, I thought, and remained standing until the minister walked in. A hush fell on the room as he took his place and turned to face the gathering and the service began.

When it finally came to the end, the coffin was sealed and I knew that I had looked at my father's face for the last time. The voice that had tormented me over the decades was finally silenced and now I could go to the graveyard to see his coffin lowered into the ground.

That day might have been the day of his funeral to everyone there, but for me it was my goodbye to Ireland. That was the last day I would go to the cemetery and that was the day that I smiled at my father's friends, who had liked his act but never known the man, for the final time. That was a grave that I would never visit and never attend to; the grass would grow over it and my parents lying together for eternity would finally be forgotten.

My father had left instructions which my mother had signed before her death that he was to share her grave. Her coffin had been dug up, covered by a mound of imitation grass to hide it from the mourners' eyes and laid by the side of the open grave. During the short ceremony at the cemetery when the coffin was lowered into the ground, I defied convention and stood beside it. My father's relatives with bowed heads took their place on the side opposite.

Only I knew that the flowers I had placed on the coffin that day, the last ones I would ever place, were for my mother. For I still mourned the woman that he had corrupted, still missed the person she could have been and still grieved for the relationship we had never had.

That day his coffin would be placed into the ground first and to my satisfaction hers would cover it. Now she would have the upper hand for eternity I thought wryly.

The short interment ceremony came to an end and the coffin was ready to be covered by the soil. My uncle had already scattered a handful on the wooden box. The following morning, the women would arrive to admire the flowers that covered the grave, testament to the popularity of the dead man.

I would not be with them.

I watched my relatives drive away and knew I would never see them again. I climbed back into the black limousine which led the convoy to the British Legion Club.

The town of Larne had done my father proud. In death he had the admiration and respect of the local people. The British Legion Club had tactfully asked for my permission to take care of all the arrangements for the after-funeral refreshments. Gratefully I had given it and, with true Irish generosity, they had laid out a magnificent spread. The wooden trestle tables which had been set up were almost groaning with the weight. The women of Larne must have worked from early morning for all the food laid out before me was, I could see, home made.

There were piles of sandwiches, small sausages, slices of pork pies in rich flaky pastry, portions of grilled chicken and bowls of fresh salads at one end, while at the other sat an assortment of homemade cakes from the lightest sponges to the rich fruit cakes so popular in my childhood. Brightly coloured hundreds and thousands were liberally dotted on the thick yellow custard which topped the sherry flavoured trifles whilst jugs of cream were placed to the side for extra cholesterol comfort. And of course there were the numerous obligatory pots of strong tea which were poured into white pottery cups by the many willing helpers.

My father's relatives were conspicuous by their absence. They had made no excuses to the local people before they left and I knew that their departure had aroused curiosity but I offered no explanation.

I felt that knowing what my father really was stopped his family mixing with people who saw him in such a different light. Maybe their wish to distance themselves from me, the last living memory, was uppermost in their minds. Whichever it was, I felt the throb of remembered pain from scars long healed and a momentary flash of that old feeling of isolation. Pushing it to one side, I went to mingle with his friends.

Stories were being told by men who had bypassed the tea in favour of the bar, stories of 'Good old Joe' and their memories of him. As the afternoon wore on, their voices got louder, their walks wider-legged and the gait more unsteady. The faces grew redder and the tales became more and more raucous. The life that my father had lived during the final years of his marriage gradually unfolded.

That day I learnt that not only was he a top amateur golfer and a brilliant snooker player but for many years before my mother had died, he had become a cup-winning ballroom dancer. In his later years it was he who had led the women on to the dance floor at the British Legion Club's monthly dances. I remembered my mother telling me of the night they had met; how he had literally swept her off her feet at a local dance hall. My mother had been bewitched and remained so for fifty years.

My shy mother, who had never felt attractive, was not the only woman my father had swept off her feet over the years of his marriage. I had guessed that but up until then I had not realized he had done it so close to home. In the buzz of conversation and the shouts of laughter and tall stories, my mother's name was absent. Only three years after her death, she was not even a shadow on their memory.

The British Legion had always been his domain; Ruth had disliked alcohol and seldom gone there. That day, only Joe was spoken about and of his wife of over fifty years, not a mention was made.

I was introduced to his dance partner and now I had a name for the elderly woman I had seen at the service. I put aside the resentment I felt on my mother's behalf at her exclusion and smiled politely.

She tearfully took my arm. 'Oh, Antoinette, you don't mind if I call you that? Your father talked about you so much I feel I know you.'

Minding desperately, I kept the smile on my face and replied, 'Nowadays I'm called Toni.'

I could not tell her that only my father ever called me by that name and that Antoinette was the name of a small frightened child, not me.

'I'm going to miss Joe so much,' she continued. 'I'm sorry, dear, you must be feeling his loss too.' With that, she gave my arm a sympathetic squeeze.

I gave her his watch which the hospital had given me. Seeing her pleasure at this memento, I knew that to her he had been someone special.

She smiled at me, clearly wanting to prolong our conversation, perhaps because I was the last link to the man who had been so important in her life. 'I'm a grandmother you know – my daughter has two little ones. They come to visit me nearly every weekend.'

I saw her face reflecting the joy that the frequent visits of those two small people gave her and felt an icy shiver through my body.

How well my father had kept his real self hidden.

Again she told me how much he would be missed, thinking I needed to hear those words for comfort. She was not to know that my loss was of those invisible bonds that had tied me to my parents. They were bonds undetectable to the naked eye but so powerful they might have been made of steel – and they were broken at last.

The day finally drew to a close and I could at last let drop the fixed smile that had been glued on my face for so many hours that my muscles ached.

I knew that my ghosts were almost put to bed and I went to talk the minister for the last time. Not only had he given me the support I so desperately needed when my mother was dying but he had eased my way through this difficult funeral. I thanked him for the hours of help he had given me.

'Do you remember when we talked three years ago at the hospice before my mother died?'

'Yes, Toni, I remember it well.' He looked at me reflectively. 'How do you feel now?'

'Drained,' I replied, 'but relieved everything is over.'

He did not ask me what I meant by that. Instead he asked, 'Will you come back? There are people here who care for you.'

'No,' I replied. 'I'm finished here.'

And I knew he understood that I wanted a complete break from my past. I thought then what I had thought once when I had been in hospital: if the people where my parents had lived could forget me, then I could forget my years in Ireland.

Later that evening I searched for that peace that I had believed the death of my father would bring. But try as I might to force myself to feel joy at being set free, I couldn't.

I tried to tell myself that no longer would I receive phone calls informing me that one of my parents was ill. No longer would I have to pretend to the people of Larne that mine had been a normal childhood and I was just a dutiful daughter returning to visit my parents in their old age. No longer would I have to listen to comments on how alike I looked to which ever parent they were talking about.

Instead, I felt emptiness, an unsettling feeling of something left undone. I picked up the car keys hoping a drive would relax me.

As though it had a mind of its own the car took me to the farmhouse which had been the last home where my parents had lived together. My mother had always been a woman who loved gardening. When she was seventy she had moved to her last home. It was an old farmhouse where not one plant or, apart from weeds, one flower grew. Once there she had spent the years up to her death creating a garden of beauty. My memories of my mother in her later age were always of her working there with a look of serenity on her face. Creating such an object of beauty had brought my mother the peace that her marriage had failed to do. After her death, when I tried to picture my mother I always saw her in that garden.

I felt a need, one I had suppressed since I had been in Larne. I wanted to walk in the garden my mother had created for the last time. I wanted to knock on the door of her last home and ask the people who lived there for their permission.

At the graveyard I had felt nothing of my mother's presence, but surely I would find it there. I did not give myself any reason for wanting to feel something from her. I just knew I wanted to picture her again as she had been the last time I had seen her there, the year before she died. She had grown frail then but on her face was a happy smile as she showed me the plants grown from seedlings she had so lovingly nurtured.

I walked towards the house with that picture foremost in my mind only to find myself looking at a freshly dug field. The builder's sign was erected and then I realized they were replacing that magical garden, she had taken over ten years to create, with tennis courts.

Let it go, Toni, the voice of my past whispered. They have gone now. She has left.

Then I thought of the prison sentence given to my father, not by the law, but by my mother. Over the next thirty years, my mother had had her revenge. She had kept her husband in a cage with bars made of guilt, punishing him remorselessly for what he had put her through and all the suffering she had endured.

Every time a programme on abuse was on the television, my mother insisted that they watch it, knowing that he squirmed in mortification. Those were the years when she turned the tables and he finally danced to her tune. For she had control at last – of the property, the bank accounts, and him.

So for thirty years he lived with guilt. For he believed to the day he died that she had never known.

And I never released him from the mental prison she created by telling him the truth. He never knew, that at six, I had told her.

No, I never revealed that. For that would have set him free.

Over the years, after I'd left Ireland as teenager, I'd found that office work did not pay well. I worked as a waitress, joined a sales force selling encyclopedias door-to-door and eventually owned my own business.

I had therapy for several years and learnt that when I confided in people I trusted, true friendship was never dented but stayed the course.

Over the years people have asked me the same question over and over again: did you forgive your parents? I neither forgave nor condemned them.

Did you hate your parents? My time in hospital and the waste of my mother's life taught me many things and one of those was that hatred affects the person who feels it. Like a corrosive acid, it burns internally, destroying lives. But the recipient of it never feels its effect.

I did not let the evil that was my father or the weakness that was my mother win by allowing that emotion to enter my life.

And the last question. Did you find happiness?

Yes, I found happiness.

THE END